DK

THE MINECRAFT

IDEAS BOOK

CREATE THE REAL WORLD IN MINECRAFT

Thomas McBrien

CONTENTS

Senior Editor Helen Murray
Senior Art Editor Anna Formanek
Additional editors Nicole Reynolds,
Catherine Saunders
Additional designers David McDonald,
Isabelle Merry, James McKeag
Senior Production Editor Jennifer Murray
Senior Production Controller Lloyd Robertson
Managing Editor Paula Regan
Managing Art Editor Jo Connor
Publishing Director Mark Searle

Written by Thomas McBrien

Inspirational builds created by CEa_TIde / Cyana,
Jonathize, Erik Löf, Frost_Beer, Guillaume Dubocage,
Jakob Grafe, Jérémie Triplet, MYodaa, Ruben Six,
Sander Poelmans, sonja firehart, and Swampbaron.
Renders by Swampbaron
Minecraft build project manager Christian Glücklich

DK would like to thank: Jay Castello, Kelsey Ranallo,
Sherin Kwan, and Alex Wiltshire at Mojang;
educational consultants David Holmes, Philip Parker,
and Giles Sparrow; Maximilian Schröder for technical
support; LS Design for design assistance; Shari Last
and Lisa Stock for editorial assistance; Julia March
for proofreading. Special thanks to Max Kavanagh.

First published in Great Britain in 2023
by Dorling Kindersley Limited
DK, One Embassy Gardens, 8 Viaduct Gardens,
London SW11 7BW

The authorised representative in the EEA is
Dorling Kindersley Verlag GmbH. Arnulfstr. 124,
80636 Munich, Germany

Page design copyright © 2023
Dorling Kindersley Limited
A Penguin Random House Company

10 9 8 7 6 5 4 3 2 1
001–333294–Oct/2023

A CIP catalogue record for this book
is available from the British Library.
ISBN: 978-0-2415-8827-7

Printed and bound in China

For the curious
www.dk.com

Minecraft.net

MIX
Paper | Supporting
responsible forestry
FSC™ C018179

This book was made with Forest
Stewardship Council™ certified
paper – one small step in DK's
commitment to a sustainable future.
For more information go to
www.dk.com/our-green-pledge

INTRODUCTION

With over 800 blocks to play with, and more being added with every update, all it takes is an idea to get creative in Minecraft. In this book you'll find more than 70 amazing ideas – all inspired by the real world around you. Before you embark on your Minecraft adventure, here are some tips for getting started.

BIG IDEAS

This book is full of inspirational ideas for you to explore. On every page you'll find lots of information and tips about Minecraft – while learning about the real world that inspired the builds, too! Keep an eye out for these boxes as you flip through the pages.

BUILDING BRIEF: Discover the key features of each build and what makes it unique.

THE REAL DEAL: Learn awesome facts about the real-world inspiration behind each build.

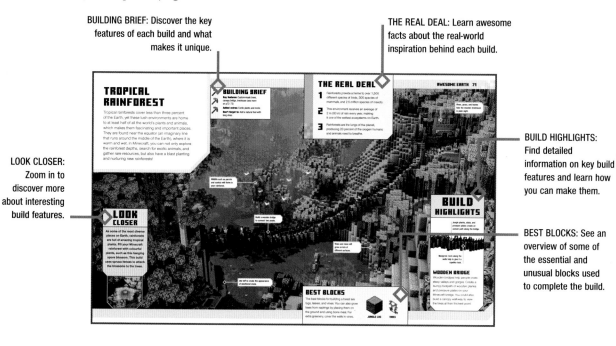

LOOK CLOSER: Zoom in to discover more about interesting build features.

BUILD HIGHLIGHTS: Find detailed information on key build features and learn how you can make them.

BEST BLOCKS: See an overview of some of the essential and unusual blocks used to complete the build.

BUILD TIP & TOP TIP: Find out cool tricks and ideas to help you improve your Minecraft building techniques.

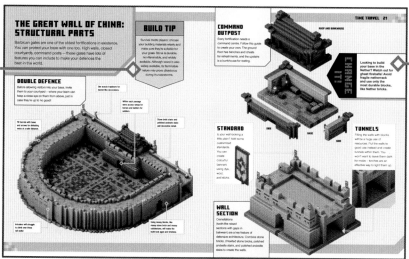

CHANGE IT!: Get ideas for how you can adapt or extend the build.

GET TO KNOW THE BLOCKS

Blocks are Minecraft's building material. They are mostly simple cubes that fill one unit of space. Together, they form your Minecraft world. They come in different shapes, sizes, and colours, and can be divided into easy-to-use groups.

BASIC BLOCKS

Most of the blocks in Minecraft are basic construction blocks. These are your primary building materials and are available in lots of different types, such as wood and stone. Many blocks are available as blocks, stairs, slabs, and walls.

REDSTONE BLOCKS

These special blocks allow you to create machines and add functioning devices, such as light switches and automatic doors, to your builds. When you dig a block of redstone you get a substance called redstone dust, which can carry power signals between items. Get familiar with these different types of redstone blocks – and harness their power in your builds!

 BLOCK **STAIRS** **WALL**

 TRAPDOOR **BUTTON** **SLAB**

 REDSTONE DUST **REDSTONE TORCH** **DROPPER** **REDSTONE REPEATER** **REDSTONE**

 POWERED RAIL **DISPENSER** **PISTON** **TARGET BLOCK**

INTERACTIVE BLOCKS

Interactive blocks, also known as utility blocks, have a purpose other than building. Some perform simple actions, like a lever, a button, or a trapdoor that opens and closes. Others are tools, such as a crafting table or furnace.

 TRAPDOOR **BUTTON** **LEVER** **ANVIL**

 CHEST **FURNACE**

 CRAFTING TABLE

 BED

COLOURS

Some blocks, like wool blocks, are available in up to 16 different colours. You can find them in your Creative inventory or craft them using dye and a crafting table.

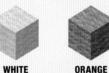 **WHITE** **ORANGE** **MAGENTA** **LIGHT BLUE**

YELLOW **LIME** **PINK** **GREY**

 LIGHT GREY **CYAN** **PURPLE** **BLUE**

BROWN **GREEN** **RED** **BLACK**

TOP TIP

The models in this book are here to inspire you. You don't have to copy them exactly. Get creative and personalize your builds. You might be inspired by a tower on a castle or to add a bubble column to your build. Or your build might look totally different!

GLOSSARY

Jumping into the world of Minecraft will introduce you to lots of new terms. Here you'll find a list of some of the terms that appear in the book and what they mean in Minecraft.

AXE
A tool used to mine wood-based blocks in Survival mode.

BANNER
A tall, decorative block that can be dyed and designed on a loom.

BIOME
A unique landscape in Minecraft, such as ocean, plains, and swamp biomes. There are more than 60 biomes in Minecraft.

BLOCK
A basic unit of structure in Minecraft occupying one unit of space.

BOOK
An item crafted with leather and paper. It can be written in or used for enchanting.

BUBBLE COLUMN
A column of water bubbles that pushes players up if made with soul sand or down if made with magma.

BUTTON
An interactive block that sends a redstone signal when pushed.

CARPET
A thin, flat layer of wool that can be dyed up to 16 colours.

COMMAND BLOCK
A special block in Minecraft that can be coded.

CRAFTING TABLE
A utility block used by Survival players to craft blocks.

CREATIVE MODE
A game mode that gives players access to an infinite supply of Minecraft's blocks and the ability to fly.

CREEPER
A hostile mob that explodes when near players.

DAYLIGHT DETECTOR
A redstone block that sends a signal when it detects light from the sky and weather.

DIMENSION
A realm in Minecraft. There are three dimensions: the Overworld, the Nether, and the End.

DOOR
An interactive barrier block that can be opened and closed with a redstone signal or by hand.

DYE
An item that can be used to change the colour of certain blocks.

ELYTRA
A pair of wings that can be found in the End dimension. Players can use it to glide through the air.

ENCHANTING TABLE
An interactive block that can be used to enchant items using experience and lapis lazuli.

ENCHANTMENT
An enhancement that can be added to a tool to improve its utility.

THE END
A dark dimension in Minecraft, characterized by the presence of the Ender Dragon and strange terrain.

END ROD
A naturally generated light source that can also be used for decoration, to climb towers, or to melt snow and ice.

FENCE
A barrier block with openings that players can see through, unlike a wall. Usually, a fence cannot be jumped over.

FENCE GATE
An interactive barrier block that cannot be jumped over and can be opened or closed by hand or with a redstone signal.

INVENTORY (CREATIVE MODE)
A pop-up menu where players can find all the available blocks.

INVENTORY (SURVIVAL MODE)
A pop-up menu where players can find their collected blocks and crafted equipment.

ITEM
One of many types of object in a player's inventory. When an item is used, a block or other entity (such as a minecart or boat) appears in the game. Items can only be displayed within the game in an item frame, a glow item frame, or an armour stand.

JOB BLOCK
A block that when placed near an unemployed villager causes them to adopt that job, such as a loom job block for a shepherd or a smoker for a butcher.

LIGHT SOURCE
A light-emitting block, such as a torch, a lantern, or a campfire.

LIGHTNING ROD
A block that redirects and protects against lightning strikes and generates a redstone signal.

LOOM
A shepherd's job block. A loom can also be used to add patterns to banners or as fuel in a furnace.

MINE
The breaking of blocks to collect resources.

MINECART
A train-like vehicle that can only be placed on a rail. Minecarts can be ridden but will stop if anything gets in their way.

MOB
A computer-controlled entity that behaves like a living creature. Mobs can be neutral, passive, or hostile.

THE NETHER
An inhospitable dimension in Minecraft.

THE OVERWORLD
A dimension in Minecraft with diverse biomes. The starting place of a player.

PICKAXE
A tool used to mine ores, rocks, and metal-based blocks in Survival mode.

PILLAGER
A hostile crossbow-wielding mob that patrols the Overworld.

PILLAR
A textured, decorative block variant.

REDSTONE
A general term for Minecraft's engineering blocks and system that allow players to create machines and add functioning devices to their builds. Also, a type of block that can be used as a redstone power source.

RESPAWNING
When players meet their end, they will respawn at their respawn location. A player can change their respawn location with a bed (Overworld) or respawn anchor (Nether).

SHEARS
A tool used to mine organic blocks in Survival mode, such as grass, leaves, and cobwebs.

SHOVEL
A tool used to mine soil-based blocks in Survival mode, such as dirt, sand, and gravel.

SLABS
A decorative block variant that is half the height of a block.

SMELTING
A method of refining blocks in Survival mode. For example, smelting will change iron ores into iron ingots.

SPAWNING
The creation of mobs and players in the game.

SPYGLASS
This magnifying tool allows players to take a closer look at objects or locations in the distance.

STAIRS
A stepped decorative block variant.

SURVIVAL MODE
A game mode where players must collect their resources and survive the dangers of day and night.

TERRAFORMING
The process of deliberately altering the environment in Minecraft, or transforming a biome into a new biome

TRADING
Exchanging emeralds and items with villagers.

TRAPDOOR
An interactive barrier block that can be opened and closed with a redstone signal or by hand.

VARIANT (OR BLOCK VARIANT)
A variation of a basic block. These include slabs, stairs, walls, trapdoors, buttons, and chiselled blocks.

VILLAGER
A passive mob that interacts with players by offering trades.

WATER SOURCE
A supply of water. Water sources can be added and moved using buckets.

XYZ LEVEL
Location coordinates in Minecraft. X indicates east and west, Z indicates north and south, and Y is height or depth in the game world.

STAYING SAFE ONLINE

It's fun to use the internet to play games, watch videos, or communicate with others, but it's important to stay safe. Here are some guidelines to follow to keep you safe when spending time online.

● Always use a username when posting something or chatting to others online (and make sure it doesn't contain your real name).

● Never give out personal information such as your name, how old you are, your phone number, or where you live.

● Never tell anyone the name or location of your school.

● Never share your password or login information with anyone (except with a parent or guardian).

● Never send personal photos to anyone.

● Always get your parent's or guardian's permission if you decide to create an account online (and remember that on many websites you need to be 13 or over to do this).

● Always tell a trusted adult if anything online has made you feel worried or uncomfortable.

BUILDING TIPS

The awesome ideas between these pages are here to inspire you to start your own project. Just remember, you must walk before you can run. Make sure to take the time to plan, research, and prepare before you start your project.

FINDING INSPIRATION

The first step to beginning a new project is finding inspiration. Look through this book, look around your town, visit the library, or even look through your holiday photos to see if there's anything you want to recreate in Minecraft. Start small and work bigger. Once you've decided on a project, focus on a small section and slowly work towards completing the full build.

DOING RESEARCH

Before you place your first block, it's important to have a plan. Do your research! What makes your idea special? Is it inspired by the real world? What details can you add to recreate the real world in Minecraft?

The SLS carries the Orion spaceship.

The SLS rocket has two rocket boosters.

It is built at a 1-block to 1-metre ratio.

EMBRACE MAKE-BELIEVE

Just like the real world has landscapes, materials, and animals, there are biomes, blocks, and mobs in Minecraft. However, sometimes you'll need to embrace the make-believe! Want a pet dog? Use a wolf! What other things can you substitute?

STARTING THE PROJECT:

Once you've chosen your idea, done your research, and decided how you will bring the real world to Minecraft, it's time to get started.

1. CHOOSE YOUR GAME MODE

CREATIVE MODE

Play Creative mode to focus on building. You will have access to an infinite supply of all the blocks in the game – and you can fly!

SURVIVAL MODE

Play Survival mode to start a Minecraft adventure. You will need to craft tools and mine for all your resources. You can build your projects, but it will be a much more challenging experience.

2. CHOOSE YOUR BEST BLOCKS

Consider your idea and choose at least five blocks that best suit it. Use these to start building. You can always add more later, but choosing five now will help you stay on track.

3. MAP YOUR AREA

Next, you need to decide where you want to build. Pick a biome. There are more than 60 to choose from. Refer to your research to pick the best one. Once you're there, prepare an area to work.

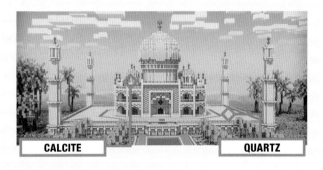

CALCITE   QUARTZ

BLOCK PLACEMENT

Placing basic blocks is easy. Simply select a block from your inventory and tap to place it on the ground or against another block. Placing interactive blocks can be more tricky. When you tap to place against an interactive block, you'll interact with it! To place a block against an interactive block, first crouch and then tap.

BLOCK DIRECTION

Some blocks can be placed to face different directions, like stairs. You can decide which direction a block is placed by rotating your character.

> **You can keep track of your building progress and even show different building stages by placing maps in item frames. Maps only update when you hold them in your hands.**
>
> **TOP TIP**

TIME TRAVEL

Humans are amazing! Over tens of thousands of years on this planet, we have created and built countless wonders. There's lots of inspiration to be found in our past. Can you recreate any of these special buildings and vehicles? Or perhaps you'll be inspired to make your own unique wonders.

GREAT PYRAMID

The Great Pyramid is the largest of three pyramids found near the ancient ruins of Memphis in Egypt. The kings and queens of Ancient Egypt, known as pharaohs, built the pyramids as homes for the afterlife, where they believed they would be reincarnated as gods. The enormous size of these structures was a symbol of the pharaoh's power and authority. Have a go at building your own dazzling pyramid, full of secret tunnels and chambers and fit for a pharaoh.

LOOK CLOSER

The Great Pyramid has three main chambers, alongside secret tunnels and sanctums. Add a secret chamber to your pyramid and decorate it with hieroglyphs. These images told the stories of the pharaohs who rested there. Record your adventures on the chamber walls using chiselled sandstone blocks.

Recreate the pyramid's triangular shape by placing blocks in a rising staircase formation. Use stair blocks to give it a smooth-yet-blocky finish.

The King's Chamber housed the pharaoh's sarcophagus. Place a chest next to it – with items you may need in your next life.

Chiselled sandstone blocks have creepers carved into them.

Early explorers named this chamber the Queen's Chamber.

Keep your treasure safe with a secret chamber that opens using hidden levers.

THE REAL DEAL

1 The Great Pyramid was built for Pharaoh Khufu over 4,500 years ago. Each block weighs an average of 2.2 tonnes (2.5 tons) and was placed by hand.

2 The pyramid is huge! It's taller than the Statue of Liberty and covers an area the size of more than 200 tennis courts!

3 The pyramid was the world's tallest building for more than 4,300 years.

SARCOPHAGUS

Pharaohs were laid to rest in a special coffin called a sarcophagus, and this build has its own special sarcophagus. In Minecraft, players can use beds to save their respawn point. Here, the bed is enclosed in the sarcophagus so you can respawn at the centre of the pyramid.

This build uses a whopping 20,000 blocks!

Use thick walls to keep you safe from exploding creepers.

Add a hidden entrance to quickly access the most important chambers.

Include interesting details like a workbench and tools to show parts of the pyramid are still being worked on.

Gold blocks and light weighted pressure plates.

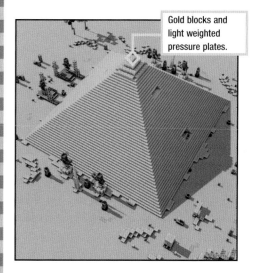

Sandstone is found widely in desert biomes. It can be found below layers of sand.

HISTORIC FACADE

Today, the Great Pyramid has the yellowish hue of sandstone, but when it was first built it shone a brilliant white. These white outer blocks disappeared over time. You can recreate the pyramid's original facade with bright blocks like quartz stairs. Experts also believe the stones at the top of the pyramid (the capstone) were covered in gold leaf.

BEST BLOCKS

If you're building in Survival mode, remember that not all the blocks can be seen from the outside of a pyramid. Collect enough sandstone and quartz for the exterior and interior walls, and fill in the rest with whatever blocks you have on hand.

SANDSTONE

QUARTZ

THE GREAT WALL OF CHINA

The Great Wall of China is the longest structure ever built by humanity. It stretches all the way from the east coast of China to the Jiayu Pass far to the west. No one knew exactly how long it was until it was measured in 2012. You can protect your base's borders with your very own great wall in Minecraft.

BUILDING BRIEF

Key features: Stone blocks, long sections of walls, guard towers, gatehouses (see more on p19–20)

Added extras: Stone block variants for extra depth

Don't forget to: Add signal campfires

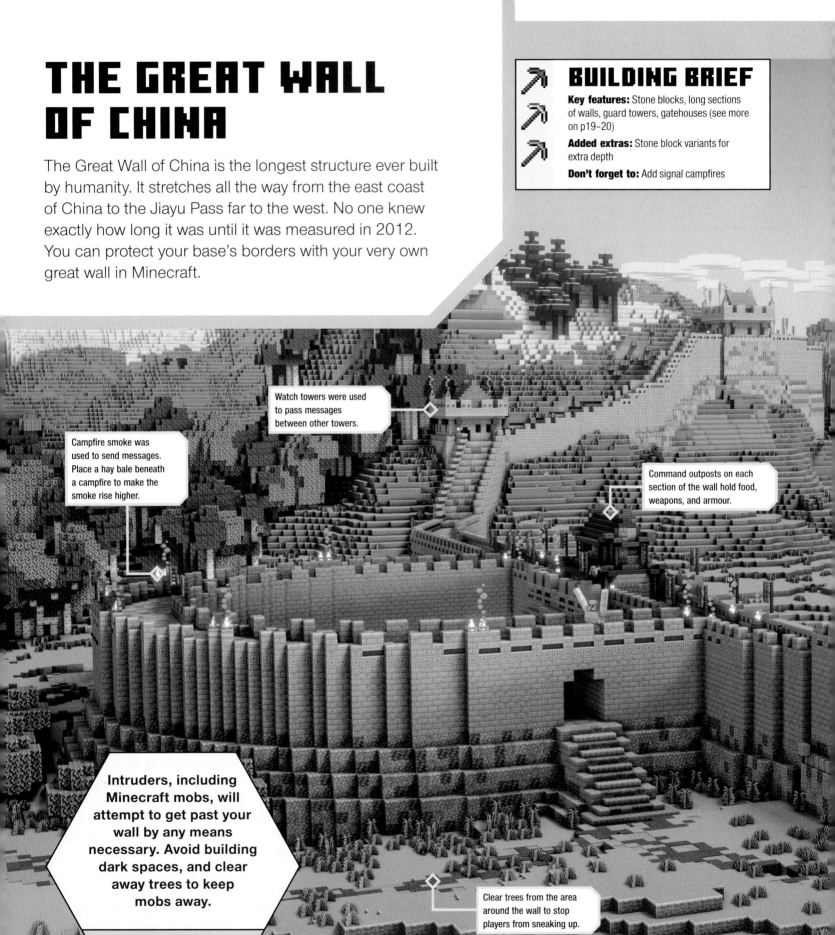

Watch towers were used to pass messages between other towers.

Campfire smoke was used to send messages. Place a hay bale beneath a campfire to make the smoke rise higher.

Command outposts on each section of the wall hold food, weapons, and armour.

Clear trees from the area around the wall to stop players from sneaking up.

Intruders, including Minecraft mobs, will attempt to get past your wall by any means necessary. Avoid building dark spaces, and clear away trees to keep mobs away.

TOP TIP

THE REAL DEAL

1 The wall was built over hundreds of years, with the earliest sections dating as far back as the 7th century BCE.

2 The full length of the wall measures over 21,000 km (13,000 miles). It's the longest structure ever built and was made a UNESCO World Heritage site in 1987.

3 Contrary to popular belief, the wall cannot be seen from the moon. This rumour started many years before anyone had even been to the moon!

BUILD HIGHLIGHTS

Want to build a great wall of your own? Pick a biome and choose blocks from around you. This wall is built within the plains biome and uses lots of stone and mossy cobblestone. You could build your wall in a badlands biome using terracotta and red sandstone instead.

Build watch towers at high points to make it easier to spot invaders.

The wall stretches over all terrain. There's no mountain too high or river too low to stop it.

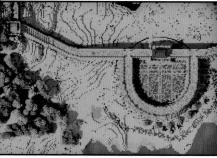

BARBICAN ENTRANCE

Semi-circular or rectangular structures were built along the wall to protect vulnerable entrances from attack.

MAP OVERVIEW

A great wall can protect everything, no matter how big your base. If the Great Wall was recreated in Minecraft at a 1:1 scale, it would be more than 21 million blocks long!

BEST BLOCKS

This plains biome has over a dozen stone variants to choose from, from cobblestone to deepslate, and crafted blocks too. Use a mix of stone blocks to give your structure character.

COBBLESTONE

MOSSY COBBLESTONE

THE GREAT WALL OF CHINA: STRUCTURAL PARTS

Barbican gates are one of the oldest fortifications in existence. You can protect your base with one too. High walls, closed courtyards, command posts — these gates have lots of features you can include to make your defences the best in the world.

BUILD TIP

Survival mode players: choose your building materials wisely and make sure they're suitable for your goals. Stone is durable, non-flammable, and widely available. Although wood is also widely available, its flammable nature may prove disastrous during thunderstorms.

DOUBLE DEFENCE

Before allowing visitors into your base, invite them to your courtyard – where your team can keep a close eye on them from above, just in case they're up to no good!

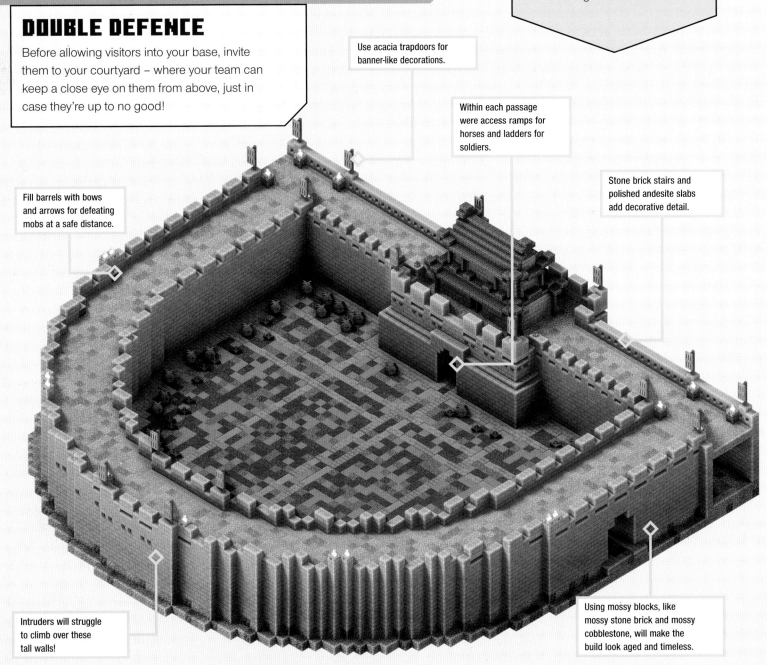

Use acacia trapdoors for banner-like decorations.

Within each passage were access ramps for horses and ladders for soldiers.

Stone brick stairs and polished andesite slabs add decorative detail.

Fill barrels with bows and arrows for defeating mobs at a safe distance.

Intruders will struggle to climb over these tall walls!

Using mossy blocks, like mossy stone brick and mossy cobblestone, will make the build look aged and timeless.

COMMAND OUTPOST

Every fortification needs a command centre. Follow this guide to create your own. The ground floor has benches and chests for refreshments, and the upstairs is a bunkhouse for resting.

ROOF AND BUNKHOUSE

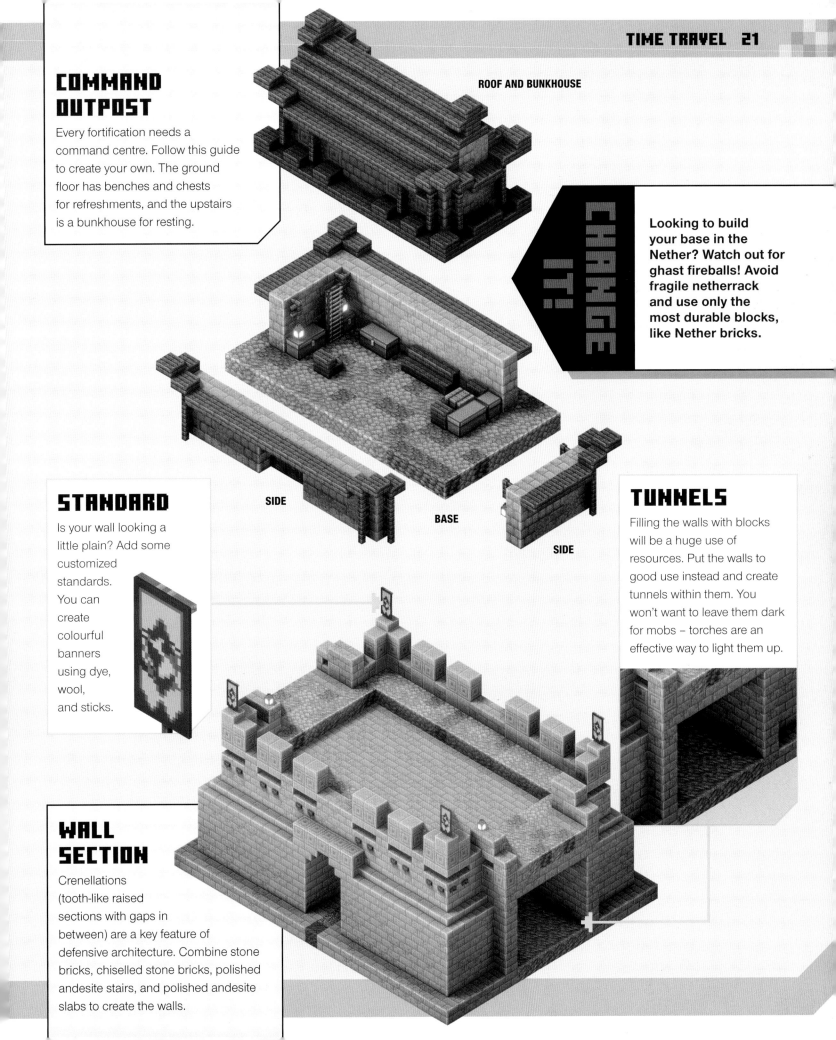

SIDE

BASE

SIDE

CHANGE IT!

Looking to build your base in the Nether? Watch out for ghast fireballs! Avoid fragile netherrack and use only the most durable blocks, like Nether bricks.

STANDARD

Is your wall looking a little plain? Add some customized standards. You can create colourful banners using dye, wool, and sticks.

TUNNELS

Filling the walls with blocks will be a huge use of resources. Put the walls to good use instead and create tunnels within them. You won't want to leave them dark for mobs – torches are an effective way to light them up.

WALL SECTION

Crenellations (tooth-like raised sections with gaps in between) are a key feature of defensive architecture. Combine stone bricks, chiselled stone bricks, polished andesite stairs, and polished andesite slabs to create the walls.

CIRCUS MAXIMUS

Ancient Romans were huge fans of public games. Crowds of spectators would fill the stands of grand stadiums like this one, the Circus Maximus. Loyal fans cheered on their favourite charioteers as they raced horse-drawn chariots at top speed. It was an exciting and dangerous sport. Why not build a grand stadium or race track and see who can gallop their horses the fastest?

Build the spectator stands in a rising staircase formation so that everyone has a good view of the track.

Circus Maximus had a decorated barrier down the middle of the track. Create your own version, using lots of colourful blocks.

Use a mix of packed mud, brown mushroom blocks, and rooted dirt to give the track a trodden texture.

Include levers on the central barrier for counting laps.

LOOK CLOSER

Safety first! Horses can jump as high as five blocks. Make sure you build tall barriers between the track and seating areas to keep spectators safe, plus a barrier down the middle of the track. When planning a games stadium, include several entrances to avoid crowding.

Chariots have basic bodies and a pair of wheels. They were drawn by up to four horses.

Arches were a key feature of Roman architecture.

Include posts to mark the point where the chariots need to turn.

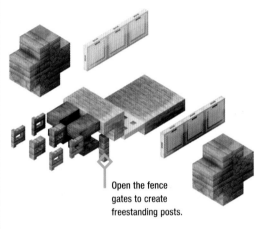

STARTING LINE

Contestants will be racing in a loop. To keep it fair, everyone needs to race an equal distance. However, going around the bend will add extra for the player closest to the stands. You could add a staggered starting line to your build to ensure everyone is on an equal footing.

Open the fence gates to create freestanding posts.

CREATE A CHARIOT

You can use your stadium for horse racing, or you could build some chariots as a nod to ancient times. Design a unique chariot, using stairs, trapdoors, anvils, and fence gates. Bring your horses to the chariot and attach them with leads.

THE REAL DEAL

1 Circus Maximus is Latin for "Biggest Circus". It was the largest entertainment venue in ancient Rome, with seating for more than 250,000 people.

2 The arena was in use for almost a millennium. Imagine how many millions of people attended a game here!

3 Charioteers were grouped into four teams: the Reds, Whites, Blues, and Greens – each with obsessive fans.

BEST BLOCKS

The Romans built using natural materials like wood and stone. To fit in with the times, build the structure using sandstone blocks. Then add the details, like seating and fences, using wood. Birch planks blend well with sandstone.

SANDSTONE

BIRCH PLANKS

THE FORBIDDEN CITY

The Imperial Palace, widely known as the Forbidden City, is a series of grand palaces in the centre of China's capital city, Beijing. Surrounded by high walls and a moat, it was home to China's emperors for almost 500 years. It got its name because most ordinary people were not allowed inside the palace compound. It has more than 8,700 rooms, including living quarters and halls, plus several gardens. Build your own palace complex in Minecraft. How will you arrange the buildings? Who will you allow to visit it?

BUILDING BRIEF

Key features: Moated and walled compound with multiple buildings

Added extras: Pagoda, Hall of Supreme Harmony (see more on p26–27)

Don't forget to: Bring cats to the palace

Build extended roofs, known as gables, to recreate a key feature of Chinese architecture.

Use stacked red sandstone walls to create narrow columns.

Pale walls contrast with the darker palace.

Add lamps – this one is a campfire held up on a hopper and mangrove wood stand.

BEST BLOCKS

Red concrete powder and the darker red Nether wart blocks are used throughout to give the Forbidden City its characteristic red colour. They are used in the walls, the roof, and even the throne room.

NETHER WART BLOCK

RED CONCRETE POWDER

THE REAL DEAL

1 The Forbidden City was finished in 1420, after 14 years of building and around one million people working on it. It is the largest palace in the world.

2 The Forbidden City is surrounded by 10-m- (35-ft-) high walls and a 52-m- (171-ft-) wide moat. It is now a museum and World Heritage Site.

3 The emperors didn't want birds spoiling their palace, so the builders made the roofs too sloping and slippery for birds to land on.

BUILD HIGHLIGHTS

The Forbidden City is an enormous complex filled with lots of palaces and pavilions. It has a consistent architectural style throughout, in terms of colours and gabled roofs. The most important buildings here are larger and ornately decorated, with grand names such as the "Hall of Supreme Harmony".

Slabs are perfect for a wide but shallow staircase.

WUFENG LOU

The entrance to the Forbidden City is guarded by the Meridian Gate. The five pavilions that overlook the entrance give the gate its nickname: Five-Phoenix Tower (Wufeng Lou in Mandarin).

There are 100 cats living at the real palace to scare off vermin such as mice. Add cats or ocelots to your build to keep creepers at bay!

Add criss-cross andesite and polished andesite to create paved flooring.

Large builds like this one use a lot of similar blocks, so plan the blocks you want to use before you start. This build uses red sandstone, warped planks, and bamboo slabs and stairs to recreate the traditional style.

TOP TIP

GABLES

The iconic gabled roofs of the Forbidden City are not held in place by nails. They're supported by dougong, a system of interlocking wooden roof brackets attached to vertical columns. In this model, the effect is recreated with stripped spruce logs, trapdoors, and fences.

THE FORBIDDEN CITY: INSIDE

The Forbidden City has three courtyards, with the Hall of Supreme Harmony in the centre. It was in these courtyards that major political decisions were made. The higher a person's social status, the deeper into the city they were allowed to go. Access to the Inner Court was generally limited to the royal family. Any visitors had to stop 20 steps from the gates and were rarely allowed in. Building this city-sized compound will need careful thought. Plan the space you need and build outwards from the centre to ensure you can fit its many palaces.

THE HALL OF SUPREME HARMONY

Holding court was the main duty expected of a ruling emperor. Court served many purposes, from lawmaking and administration to coronations, weddings and other important ceremonies. The Hall of Supreme Harmony was built for the most special of occasions. Will you give any of your buildings a special purpose?

HEAT

Braziers provide outdoor heat and lighting, so place them in the area in front of the pavilion. They can be made using a campfire, mangrove trapdoors, and an andesite wall.

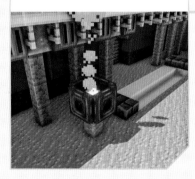

Recreate the pavilion roof with red concrete powder, red terracotta, bamboo slabs, and stairs.

Install windows using spruce fences.

Use quartz slabs, deepslate brick slabs, and calcite for a grand staircase.

Complete the walls using white concrete powder, calcite, and smooth quartz stairs.

The Forbidden City reflects traditional Chinese architecture. What do the buildings near where you live look like? Build your own palace in any style that you like – old or new.

CHANGE IT!

Yellow was the emperor's colour in Imperial China – bamboo is a perfect fit in Minecraft.

Imperial banquets are held at the Hall of Preserving Harmony.

The Hall of Medium Harmony is a pagoda. Here, it stands on a large andesite platform.

The Hall of Supreme Harmony was used for ceremonial events. New emperors were crowned here.

BRIDGES

The Golden Water River snakes through the first courtyard, crossed by five white stone bridges bringing visitors from the Meridian Gate into the heart of the Outer Courtyard. These Minecraft bridges are made from smooth quartz, iron trapdoors, birch wall signs, and birch trapdoors.

PAGODA

Pagodas are characterized by their tiered roofs. This Minecraft version uses bamboo slabs and stairs and spruce trapdoors to create two closely connected, tiered gables.

Gate of Supreme Harmony

Golden Water River

OUTER COURT

Anyone deemed important enough to be allowed into the Forbidden City would first find themselves in the Outer Court. This was the centre of Chinese politics, where all the most powerful people in China came to make laws or ask for the emperor's help.

There are no trees in the Outer Court, perhaps to make it easier to defend.

Meridian Gate

POLYNESIAN VOYAGING CANOE

Polynesians have a long history of navigation. They are believed to be the first people to navigate through long stretches of open water. Using the stars, wind patterns, and wildlife, they sailed their outrigger canoes to islands throughout the Polynesian Triangle – that's thousands of kilometres of ocean! Set off on your own grand voyage in Minecraft, using only the stars and clouds to navigate.

BUILDING BRIEF

Key features: Wooden outrigger, colourful sails

Added extras: Add a Minecraft boat to the canoe to use as a dinghy

Don't forget to: Pack fishing rods and a cauldron for fresh drinking water

TOP TIP

You can use compass directions in Minecraft. The sun and moon rise in the east and set in the west. Stars also follow the east-west pattern of the sun and moon. Clouds always float west.

Add a cauldron for collecting fresh drinking water.

Polynesians caught turtles, fish, and other marine life.

BEST BLOCKS

The Polynesians relied on available resources to build their boats, like trees. As you travel to new islands you can collect different wooden blocks like birch, mangrove, and spruce to build with.

STRIPPED MANGROVE LOG

STRIPPED SPRUCE LOG

STRIPPED BIRCH LOG

THE REAL DEAL

1 Polynesian outriggers were very sturdy. They could navigate journeys of up to 4,800 km (3,000 miles).

2 Polynesia extends from New Zealand in the south all the way to Hawaii in the north, and as far out as Easter Island in the east.

3 Historically, Polynesian navigators made their own maps using sticks, shells, and coconut fibres.

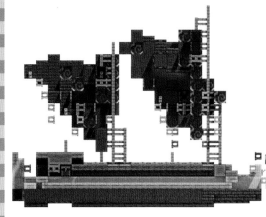

OUTRIGGER SHAPE

Outriggers are formed by adding an elevated platform on top of two canoes. The small gap between the canoes allows it to sail faster as there is less resistance from the water. In Minecraft, the boat's platform is made with lots of trapdoors with a small storage space below. Trapdoors are very flat blocks that help the boat appear extra lightweight.

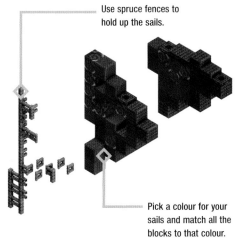

Use spruce fences to hold up the sails.

Pick a colour for your sails and match all the blocks to that colour.

Use tripwires to look like the ropes that secure sails in place.

The large canoes had space to carry supplies and goods, allowing groups and families to undertake long voyages to new islands.

Use a mix of different wood types, like oak and spruce, for a colourful finish.

The outrigger floats atop two long wooden canoes. Use stripped mangrove logs to look like carved tree trunks.

SAILS

The big sails on outrigger canoes were used to catch the wind. Polynesians crafted their sails using plaited mats of palm-like pandanus leaves, while the cords connecting them were made from coconut fibres. These Minecraft sails use wool, glazed red terracotta, and mangrove planks instead. Experiment with different blocks to create sails in your favourite colours.

NEUSCHWANSTEIN CASTLE

The picturesque conical towers of Neuschwanstein Castle are a familiar sight to many – this is the castle that inspired Disney's Cinderella Castle. It was built for Ludwig II of Bavaria, Germany, a rich ruler who wanted to live in a fairytale castle filled with images of his favourite legends. And after 17 years of construction, he did. Luckily, this Minecraft Neuschwanstein Castle is just as full of magic, but doesn't take nearly as long to build.

Add exterior details to your castle. The real Neuschwanstein has a painting of St George slaying the dragon.

BUILDING BRIEF

Key features: Conical towers, grand courtyards, gatehouses

Added extras: Mountaintop with trees

Don't forget to: Light up the woods to keep hostile mobs away

Decorate your Minecraft castle with your very own flags atop the tallest towers. Use anvils and diorite walls to create the flagpole and then place iron bars above them. You can then create flags using dyed wool blocks.

CHANGE IT!

Place your castle atop a mountain to represent the beautiful, craggy Bavarian mountains.

BEST BLOCKS

As a fairytale castle in the Bavarian mountains, it's only natural that it should feature the most elegant blocks. The main buildings of this Minecraft version use quartz blocks with occasional diorite blocks for defining features. Birch planks are also used for their golden appearance.

QUARTZ

DIORITE

BIRCH PLANKS

THE REAL DEAL

1 Neuschwanstein Castle might look like a medieval castle, but it was actually built in the 19th century.

2 Ludwig II was a huge fan of legends and fairytales. Throughout the castle, there are paintings of knights, texts from poets and kings, and statues of swans. The castle's name means "new swan stone".

3 Despite the castle being built for just Ludwig II and his servants, he had planned for there to be over 200 rooms. He died before most were completed.

This square tower provides a contrast to the round towers of the main palace.

Light campfires along the road to keep snow from collecting on the ground.

Add a red brick gatehouse overlooking the castle entrance.

Use stone and andesite to give the entrance the appearance of being carved from the mountain.

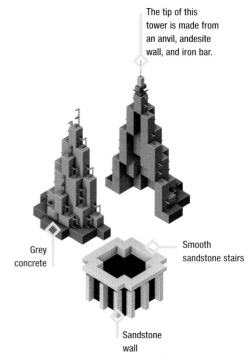

The tip of this tower is made from an anvil, andesite wall, and iron bar.

Grey concrete

Smooth sandstone stairs

Sandstone wall

CONICAL ROOF

Have you ever built a conical roof? They look just like ice-cream cones. Start by building one half of the roof to get the shape, then mirror it to complete it. When its done, add some fun details to the very top. The roofs in this model include lots of grey stained-glass panes that make them appear smooth from a distance.

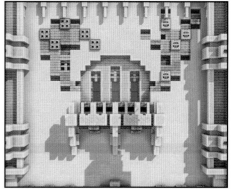

COLOURFUL WINDOWS

Ludwig used stained glass to decorate the royal bedrooms. Add blue stained glass to symbolize the Bavarian flag, or choose your favourite colours for your own fairytale castle.

FASIL GHEBBI

The fortress of Fasil Ghebbi is located in Gondar, Ethiopia. Its mighty castle, Enqualal Gemb, provides incredible inspiration for any builder looking to protect themselves from hostile neighbours. With huge towers, a long ramp, and tall battlements, this castle will make any would-be assailants think twice before launching a raid. What will you add to your base to protect it from roaming pillagers?

THE REAL DEAL

1 Fasil Ghebbi was founded in the 17th century by the Ethiopian emperor Fasilides. It was home to the country's emperors until the 18th century.

2 Fasil Ghebbi is a fortress-city that features palaces, churches, and monasteries.

3 The walls of the fortress are made of large, tall stones. They are still standing today, despite being over 400 years old.

Make battlements from jungle planks and jungle stairs.

Use wall blocks in corners to create protective narrow windows.

Windows are secured behind dark oak trapdoors.

The fortress of Fasil Ghebbi has a mix of Arab, Hindu, and European architecture styles. The castle has four towers topped with Arab-style domes. Use walls instead of blocks for the domes in your Minecraft version to achieve a more rounded, less bulky effect.

LOOK CLOSER

Build the castle with sturdy granite blocks. Add some jungle planks to give the walls an interesting texture.

BATTLEMENTS

Battlements have small gaps in the walls that allow archers to shoot arrows while giving them cover from return fire. Create these in Minecraft using jungle planks and jungle stairs. Keep a chest of arrows on top of your castle to use when fighting off raiding pillagers. It is also the perfect place to store cauldrons of water. They can be used to put out fires before the blocks burn down.

ENTRY RAMP

The main entrance to the castle is via this ramp. Make your ramp extra long using slabs instead of stairs. The basement entrance of the fortress can be barricaded with durable blocks, such a granite and dripstone, to force castle invaders up the narrow ramp. This will leave attacking mobs exposed, and you can rain arrows down on them from the battlements!

BEST BLOCKS

Creating a secure structure means building with durable blocks. Try to use as many stone-type blocks as possible, such as granite, mud bricks, and dripstone.

DRIPSTONE   **MUD BRICKS**   **GRANITE**

RMS TITANIC

The RMS *Titanic* was one of the largest and most luxurious ships of the 20th century. Its ten decks were fitted with everything its passengers could need to keep them entertained during the week-long voyage from Southampton, England, to New York, USA. The ship's special watertight design led newspapers to name it the "unsinkable ship", but they were sadly very wrong about that. Why not create this opulent ship in Minecraft – or build another grand ship of your own?

BUILDING BRIEF

Key features: Luxury steamship with four smokestacks plus rooms, restaurants, and lounges inside (see more on p36–37)

Added extras: Cargo decoration

Don't forget to: Add lots of ornate details

TOP TIP

Teamwork makes the dream work! Check out the guide on p36–37 and ask your friends to help you build your own luxury cruise ship. Start with the basic ship structure before moving on to the different rooms.

The original *Titanic* didn't have enough lifeboats, so make sure you're well prepared in your version.

Large windows capture the sea breeze. Add iron trapdoors to close them during storms.

Use red terracotta blocks to mark the waterline, which is the level normally reached by water on the side of a boat.

Install a bell for emergencies. Ring it to warn passengers.

THE REAL DEAL

1 The *Titanic* sank on April 15, 1912, on its maiden (first) voyage after hitting an iceberg in the Atlantic Ocean.

2 The enormous ship was more than 269 m (882 ft) long. That's the length of 22 buses lined up end to end!

3 The *Titanic* had four smokestacks, but only three of them were functional. Smokestacks make a ship look powerful, so the builders added an extra fake one.

BUILD HIGHLIGHTS

The *Titanic* earned itself a place in history for its gigantic size. This enormous recreation strives to match the scale of the original build. It is 193 blocks long and 53 blocks tall!

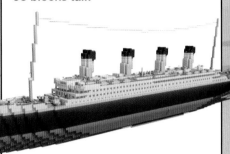

SMOKESTACKS

The *Titanic*'s smokestacks (also known as funnels) were built at an angle to help smoke billow into the sky. In Minecraft, this effect can be achieved by placing blocks in a zig-zag formation.

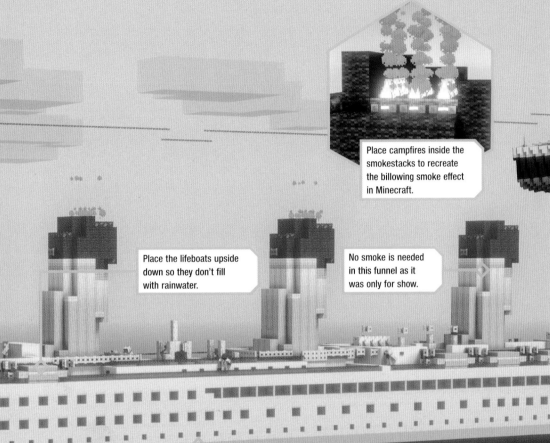

Place campfires inside the smokestacks to recreate the billowing smoke effect in Minecraft.

Place the lifeboats upside down so they don't fill with rainwater.

No smoke is needed in this funnel as it was only for show.

Create small windows using smooth quartz stairs instead of blocks.

DECK

Keeping a ship sailing takes a lot of equipment and supplies. Add cranes for loading cargo – these are made from polished diorite and diorite wall blocks. The cargo hold entrance has been recreated here using daylight detectors.

BEST BLOCKS

This enormous build uses lots of different blocks. To create the basic shape of the ship you will need lots of smooth quartz, black wool, and red terracotta, plus oak slabs for the decks.

RED TERRACOTTA

OAK SLABS

SMOOTH QUARTZ

RMS TITANIC: SHIP BUILDING

Bigger than three football fields and with room for more than 3,300 passengers and crew, the RMS *Titanic* was a magnificent ship. Recreating this vessel in all its glory is a big task in Minecraft. Will you go for historical accuracy, like this model, or design a sleeker, more modern ship?

SHIP SHAPE

This *Titanic* recreation is of an enormous scale. Before you can get down to the little details that make it so special, you'll need to master building the main shape of the boat.

BUILD TIP

The *Titanic* sits several blocks below the water's surface. This means that once you've built the hull (or main body), you'll need to empty it of water. Luckily, there's a block that makes this quick! Grab some sponges and use them to soak up the water. You can then put them in a furnace to dry and reuse them.

SPONGE

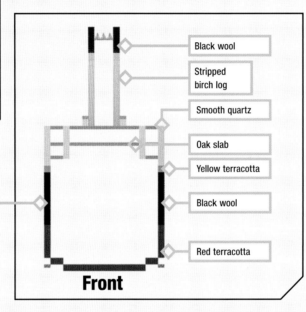

Black wool

Stripped birch log

Smooth quartz

Oak slab

Yellow terracotta

Black wool

Red terracotta

19 blocks wide and 36 blocks tall

Front

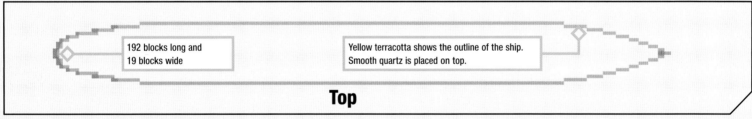

192 blocks long and 19 blocks wide

Yellow terracotta shows the outline of the ship. Smooth quartz is placed on top.

Top

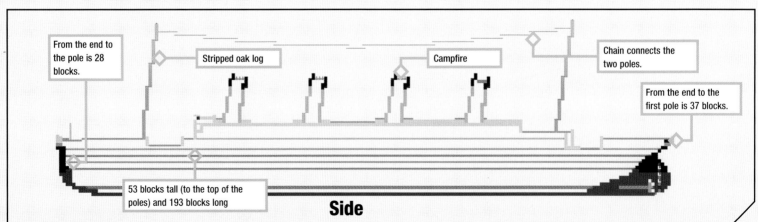

From the end to the pole is 28 blocks.

Stripped oak log

Campfire

Chain connects the two poles.

From the end to the first pole is 37 blocks.

53 blocks tall (to the top of the poles) and 193 blocks long

Side

MULTI-STOREY SHIP

The *Titanic* was taller than most buildings. The engines were in the base of the ship while the upper decks were divided into first-, second-, and third-class facilities. You can fit these floors into your Minecraft build too. Here, the upper floor first-class cabins are taller than the second-class cabins and the even more cramped third-class cabins.

FIRST CLASS

First-class passengers expect the best. This Minecraft first-class cabin has luxurious fittings including art on the walls, bookshelves, and a colourful rug (made from copper blocks!) next to the fireplace.

First-class cabins are 2.5 blocks tall.

Use slabs to make floors, to maximize the space available for cabins.

Fill the first- and second-class rooms with artwork. There are 26 paintings to choose from.

Place barrels in the walls to add discreet storage. Unlike chests, they don't need extra space to open.

Second-class cabins are 2 blocks tall.

The ship walls are 1 block thick.

The cramped third-class beds are made with red wool and a white carpet.

ENGINES

The engine room was the biggest part of the ship. The *Titanic* had three engines, recreated here using blast furnaces, stone, andesite stairs, levers, and iron bars. Place a lava bucket in the furnace to keep it burning for a long time.

Third-class cabins are 1.5 blocks tall – in Minecraft that's the smallest space you can still move around in!

First-class passengers had access to a swimming pool. Create one with water blocks.

THE HANGING GARDENS OF BABYLON

The spectacular Hanging Gardens of Babylon are thought to have existed more than 2,600 years ago, in present-day Iraq. According to legend, the gardens were a masterpiece, full of lush trees and waterways. But no remains have ever been found, so nobody knows what they really looked like. This means you can be as imaginative as you like with your Minecraft version. Which plants will you include in yours?

BUILDING BRIEF

Key features: Hanging vines, waterways, tiered terraces

Added extras: Colourful trees and vegetation

Don't forget to: Add a variety of animals and plants

LOOK CLOSER

The walls are filled with creative designs that let in lots of natural light. Using a mix of stairs, slabs, and blocks with different textures you can create lots of fun and unique designs for your walls.

Glazed terracotta is perfect for bursts of colour. Use orange, pink, yellow, cyan, and red glazed terracotta to create colourful trees.

BEST BLOCKS

This version of the gardens uses the earthy colours of granite and ancient debris to capture the natural world setting. It's overflowing with ferns, moss, leaves, and vines.

GRANITE

ANCIENT DEBRIS

MOSS

THE REAL DEAL

1 The gardens were named one of the Seven Wonders of the World, a list of the most amazing human-made structures, which was compiled by ancient Greek travellers.

2 Ancient legend says that the gardens were built by King Nebuchadnezzar II as a gift to his queen, Amytis. They imitated the mountains of her homeland in Persia.

3 Experts have questioned whether the gardens existed because no remains have been found. Recent research suggests they did exist, but north of Babylon.

Canals and waterways look beautiful, but also provide the plants with all they need to flourish.

Decorate the gardens with ornate statues of animals.

Add campfires to fill your gardens with light.

Glazed terracotta blocks have unique textures on each side. Play around with them to create your own tree designs.

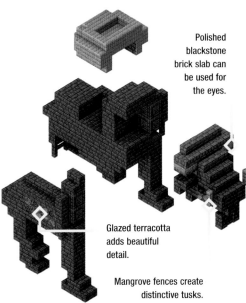

Polished blackstone brick slab can be used for the eyes.

Glazed terracotta adds beautiful detail.

Mangrove fences create distinctive tusks.

STUNNING STATUES

Majestic statues will draw in visitors to your gardens. Create elephant statues, like these, using crimson wood and Nether brick variants. This one is 10 blocks long, 6 blocks wide, and 8 blocks tall. Don't forget to recreate the large feet that help keep the elephant stable.

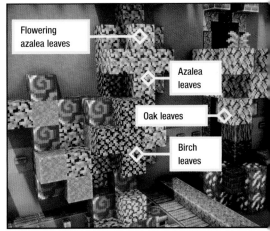

Flowering azalea leaves

Azalea leaves

Oak leaves

Birch leaves

GARDEN DESIGN

This build has lots of plants climbing up the walls. They're made from azalea, birch leaves, and oak leaves. These sorts of plants might be called creepers, but the only explosions here are the explosions of colour provided by the red glazed terracotta.

STONEHENGE

Built over 5,000 years ago in Wiltshire, England, this prehistoric marvel of epic proportions is Europe's most famous Stone Age monument. Stonehenge is still standing today and provides a meeting place for celebrations on special days of the year. Be inspired to create your own awe-inspiring monument as a place to gather with your friends.

 BUILDING BRIEF

Key features: Circle of standing stones in a grassy field

Added extras: Fallen stones

Don't forget to: Use easily available resources

A trilithon is a structure of two large vertical stones supporting a third stone set horizontally across the top.

Since Stonehenge has fallen to ruin, some blocks should look broken and scattered.

Visitors may mistake this for abandoned ruins. In fact, many of Stonehenge's blocks were taken to build nearby churches. Place a sign to keep your build safe, using a glow ink sac to make it visible at night.

TOP TIP

THE REAL DEAL

1 Stonehenge's stones align with sunrise on the longest day and sunset on the shortest days of the year (known as the summer solstice and the winter solstice).

2 Nobody knows exactly why Stonehenge was created, but historians believe it was likely used for ritual purposes linked to the changing seasons, the sun, and the sky.

3 Today, thousands still gather at Stonehenge for ceremonies to celebrate the summer and winter solstices.

HERE COMES THE SUN

Ancient builders carefully placed the stones to align with the point on the horizon where the sun rose on the summer solstice, the longest day of the year. In its own way, Stonehenge is an ancient calendar. Why not build your monument to frame the sunrise or moonrise?

> Without wheels, Stone Age builders used ingenious ways to place the rocks, such as pulley and rope systems.

> Experts believe Stonehenge once had two more trilithons standing. Some have suggested that these supported a roof.

EARLY BUILD

Many of the stones have fallen, but it is thought that Stonehenge once held as many as 165 megaliths (giant stones). You can see more of these in place in the build above. Why not recreate the Stonehenge of thousands of years ago? If you're low on cobblestone, you can simply dig underground to collect more and create stone by smelting it. Or you could use a pickaxe with Silk Touch enchantments to mine stone directly. Some experts think Stonehenge may have had a thatched roof with a wooden frame, so you could try adding a roof using wood and hay bales.

BEST BLOCKS

This is a Stone Age structure, so it's unsurprising that that the building block used is stone. However, the original build may have used all sorts of available materials, such as wood and straw, so you can experiment with different blocks, too.

STONE

STATUE OF LIBERTY

This colossal copper statue stands proud at 93 m (305 ft) tall in New York Harbor. France gave "Lady Liberty" to the USA as a gift of friendship to celebrate the 100th anniversary of the signing of America's Declaration of Independence. The striking monument was unveiled in 1886, and it told arriving immigrants that they would soon be in the land of freedom. Create your own stupendous statue to greet visitors to your Minecraft world.

BUILDING BRIEF

Key features: Copper body, flaming torch, crown, huge pedestal

Added extras: Different copper variants to highlight the changing colour of the copper

Don't forget to: Use a honeycomb to wax the copper!

THE REAL DEAL

1 New York's most famous statue originally operated as a lighthouse to guide ships home.

2 The statue's full name is "Liberty Enlightening the World", and it was created to celebrate the American Revolution and the end of slavery in the USA. The torch represents lighting the path towards freedom.

3 They say lightning doesn't strike the same spot twice... but that's not true! It is estimated that the Statue of Liberty gets struck by lightning around 600 times a year.

BUILD HIGHLIGHTS

OXIDATION

The Statue of Liberty was originally a shiny reddish-brown. Due to exposure to rain and oxygen over time, this copper colour became green in a process known as oxidation. This happens to Minecraft's copper blocks, too. Copper has four stages: copper, exposed copper, weathered copper, and oxidized copper.

Light-emitting shroomlights in the torch give the effect that it's really lit. The real torch is coated in gold.

CHANGE IT!

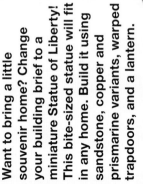

Want to bring a little souvenir home? Change your building brief to a miniature Statue of Liberty! This bite-sized statue will fit in any home. Build it using sandstone, copper and prismarine variants, warped trapdoors, and a lantern.

BEST BLOCKS

This monument is made almost exclusively of two types of blocks: sandstone and copper. All the variants have been used to add architectural details and to show the changing colour of the copper.

SANDSTONE

COPPER

The green layer on the surface of copper is known as a "patina".

Want to see how the Statue of Liberty changed over time? Build your model with unwaxed copper and watch as it slowly turns from brown to green.

You'll need lots of stacks of sandstone to build this enormous pedestal! It raises the statue high in the air to be seen from all around.

Buttons can be a final touch to any build. Here, they add more depth to the walls.

The real pedestal is set within the walls of an old army fort.

A mix of stairs, slabs, and wall block variants packs the build with lots of eye-catching details.

Use sandstone and birch block variants for the tall columns, which recreate the statue's grand neoclassic architecture style.

Coat your copper blocks with a honeycomb waxing if you want to stop them from changing colour over time. You will need to use an axe on the blocks if you wish to remove the wax.

TOP TIP

ACROPOLIS OF ATHENS

In ancient times, sturdy fortresses were built on the top of hills to protect people from invaders. Cities often sprang up around these fortresses. This Minecraft model represents one of the most famous fortresses, the Acropolis in Athens, Greece. Built in a desert biome, it recreates the famous Parthenon temple, plus many other buildings and temples, and is primarly built from sandstone.

BUILDING BRIEF

Key features: A walled fortress on top of a hill with many buildings and temples (see more on p46–47)

Added extras: A 9-block-tall statue of Athena

Don't forget to: Build a staircase to the base of the mountain

Use quartz pillar blocks to recreate the ridged columns of the Erechtheion.

Legend has it that one tree on the Acropolis was planted by Athena herself.

This nine-block-tall statue of Athena is made from waxed copper, acacia variants, and four blocks of gold.

Use yellow End stone bricks from the End dimension to create high walls.

THE REAL DEAL

1 The Acropolis in Athens was built more than 2,500 years ago.

2 Although most of the Acropolis is now in ruins, this important archaeological and heritage site has still revealed many details about how the ancient Greeks lived.

3 One of the most intact parts of the Acropolis is the Parthenon. It was a temple dedicated to the goddess Athena, after whom the city is named.

BEST BLOCKS

All eight sandstone block variants have been used in this build, so stock up on sandstone. Or head to the End dimension to collect End stone bricks for an ancient-looking, yellow alternative to sandstone.

END STONE BRICKS

RED SANDSTONE

SANDSTONE

Use red sandstone slabs and stairs to create the sloping roof of the Parthenon and other buildings.

There are eight sandstone variants, so try to use all of them in your build. Mix and match your sandstone to add edges, layers, and texture to your build. This build uses red sandstone variants to make the roofs stand out.

TOP TIP

BUILD HIGHLIGHTS

LOCATION, LOCATION

As with the real Acropolis, a strategic location is key. Find a tall sandstone outcrop in a desert biome and then flatten the top to create a large area to build on. Think about where your different buildings should go and then build high walls all around to keep the inhabitants safe from invaders. Build a steep and heavily-guarded staircase alongside the mountain to reach the fortress.

Ladders replicate carved details on the Propylaia, the ceremonial gateway to the Acropolis.

Recreate the four-column structure of the Temple of Athena Nike.

Use different blocks, such as birch slabs, to add texture to the flooring.

Add monuments, like the Pedestal of Agrippa, which stands on the stairway to the Propylaia.

Slab steps lead up the mountainside into the Acropolis.

ACROPOLIS: TEMPLES

The Acropolis of Athens began as a fortress to protect the city, but its scenic position overlooking the city made it a popular place for other buildings too, such as temples. Like many religious buildings, the Greek temples stand out from the other buildings due to their stunning design and ornate decorations. Here's how to recreate them in Minecraft, but, as always, you can always add your own ideas and unique twists to any build.

FRIEZE

The friezes on the temples were painted in blue, red, and gold, but the paint has long since worn away. Restore the temples to their former glory by using textured glazed terracotta blocks in your Minecraft versions.

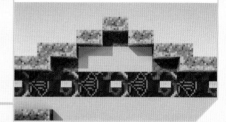

ERECHTHEION

The Erechtheion, also known as the Temple of Athena, is located on the north side of the Acropolis. It's the only non-symmetrical temple in the Acropolis. It is held up by both tall and short columns. Use ladders, trapdoors, and wall blocks to make each column unique.

Use stair blocks to make the diagonal roof. You can change the shape of a stair block by rotating your character's position.

Glazed terracotta blocks have unique patterns – unlike any other blocks in Minecraft.

CARVINGS

The walls and tops of columns in the Acropolis had intricate carvings that told stories of conquest and religion. Use chiselled sandstone to add designs to your Minecraft temple walls.

Smelt sandstone in a furnace to create smooth sandstone.

BUILD TIP

Each of the temples is sheltered beneath red sandstone roofs. You could also use acacia for these. The roofs' triangular shapes are easy to recreate with slabs and stairs. First create a ring of blocks around the temple to get the basic shape. Then slowly build upwards, diagonally, moving one or two blocks in at each level until you've created the triangular shape.

PARTHENON

Carved out of 22,000 tonnes (21,650 tons) of marble, the Parthenon is one of the world's most famous buildings. To recreate this impressive building in Minecraft, you'll need to build a cuboid sitting on a diagonal, rectangular base before adding classic Greek architectural details.

The very top of the temple is completed with lecterns and trapdoors.

Statues on the roof tell the story of Athena's birth. These Minecraft statues use fences, trapdoors, and sandstone walls and are set against a green prismarine background.

The inner walls use the same End stone bricks as the defensive Acropolis walls.

Sandstone slabs and stairs create an alcove for the statues.

COLUMNS

Columns were a key feature of ancient Greek architecture. This Minecraft model uses birch trapdoors and birch fence gates to create the details at the base and top.

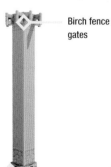

Birch fence gates

Birch trapdoor

Make the temple higher than the other buildings to emphasize its importance. Use stair blocks to raise it.

INTERIOR

Building in Minecraft can be a fun way to explore history. Did you know the Parthenon once had a statue of Athena made of gold and ivory inside? How would you create it in Minecraft?

This statue represents Athena. It uses copper blocks and stairs for the main body.

THE TAJ MAHAL

This beautiful building in Agra, India, is covered in white marble and is considered one of the New Seven Wonders of the World. The building of the Taj Mahal began in 1632 on the order of the Mughal Emperor Shah Jahan to honour his deceased wife Mumtaz. Inside, it is decorated with colourful gems arranged into intricate patterns. In Minecraft, you can build something *for* your favourite person or, even better, *with* them. It could be a magnificent palace, like the Taj Mahal, or a totally new, unique build.

BUILDING BRIEF

Key features: Square base, large central dome, four smaller domes, four tall towers (minarets)

Added extras: Rectangular pool in front, gardens on each side

Don't forget to: Add ornaments to the top of the domes

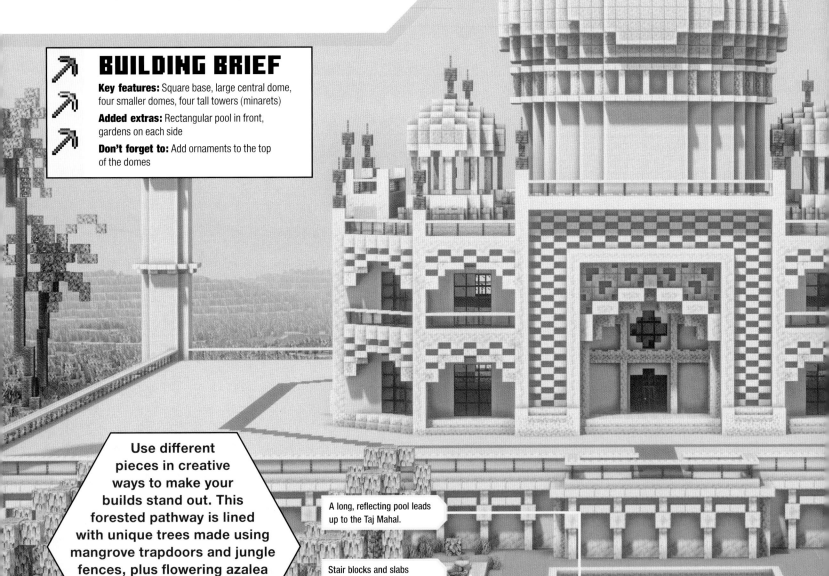

The central dome is often called the "onion dome" because of its shape.

A long, reflecting pool leads up to the Taj Mahal.

Stair blocks and slabs give the gardens a slightly tiered effect.

TOP TIP

Use different pieces in creative ways to make your builds stand out. This forested pathway is lined with unique trees made using mangrove trapdoors and jungle fences, plus flowering azalea leaves and mangrove leaves.

THE REAL DEAL

1 Over 40 different types of gemstones decorate the interior of the Taj Mahal, including diamonds, emeralds, and amethysts.

2 It took more than 20,000 workers to build the Taj Mahal and more than 20 years to build it. Minecraft building is much faster!

3 Building materials for the Taj Mahal came from all over Asia, and many of them were transported by elephants.

Use polished diorite stairs and iron trapdoors for rimmed details.

The walls use quartz bricks, smooth quartz, and polished diorite.

It's 40 blocks tall from base to tip.

MIGHTY MINARETS

Four tall, narrow minarets stand around the Taj Mahal. Minarets are often part of a mosque. Near the top is a balcony where someone called the muezzin calls people to prayer. The top of this Minecraft minaret is 11 blocks high and 5 blocks wide, and is made of diorite and deepslate block variants.

Create four minarets crowned with a *chhatri*, a decorated canopy.

The Taj Mahal is built to be perfectly symmetrical, which symbolized power in Mughal leadership.

Add trees to make beautiful gardens lining the pathway.

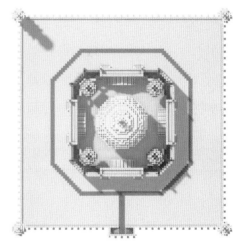

SYMMETRICAL PLAN

Looking at this Minecraft Taj Mahal from above, you can see that it is symmetrical. If there was a line through the centre, it would look exactly the same on each side, a mirror image. Four minarets are equally spaced apart with a dome in the centre. Before starting, take the time to plan your build. Splitting your build into symmetrical sections will help you stay organized.

BEST BLOCKS

The pure white marble of the Taj Mahal has faded over time. This Minecraft build reflects that, with smooth quartz blocks plus lighter-coloured diorite and calcite blocks for contrast.

SMOOTH QUARTZ

DIORITE

CALCITE

TIGER'S NEST

This isolated mountaintop monastery in the Himalayas is the perfect place to be alone with your thoughts. Tiger's Nest was built in 1692 in Bhutan as a place of worship and meditation for Buddhist monks. Known in the local language of Dzongkha as Paro Taktsang, the monastery is built halfway up a steep mountain and is nestled into the stone, making it very difficult to get to. Build a hidden, peaceful place in the mountains to visit when you would like a quiet moment to yourself.

BUILDING BRIEF

Key features: Steep mountain cliffside

Added extras: A supply cart from the base of the mountain

Don't forget to: Create a pathway leading up the mountain

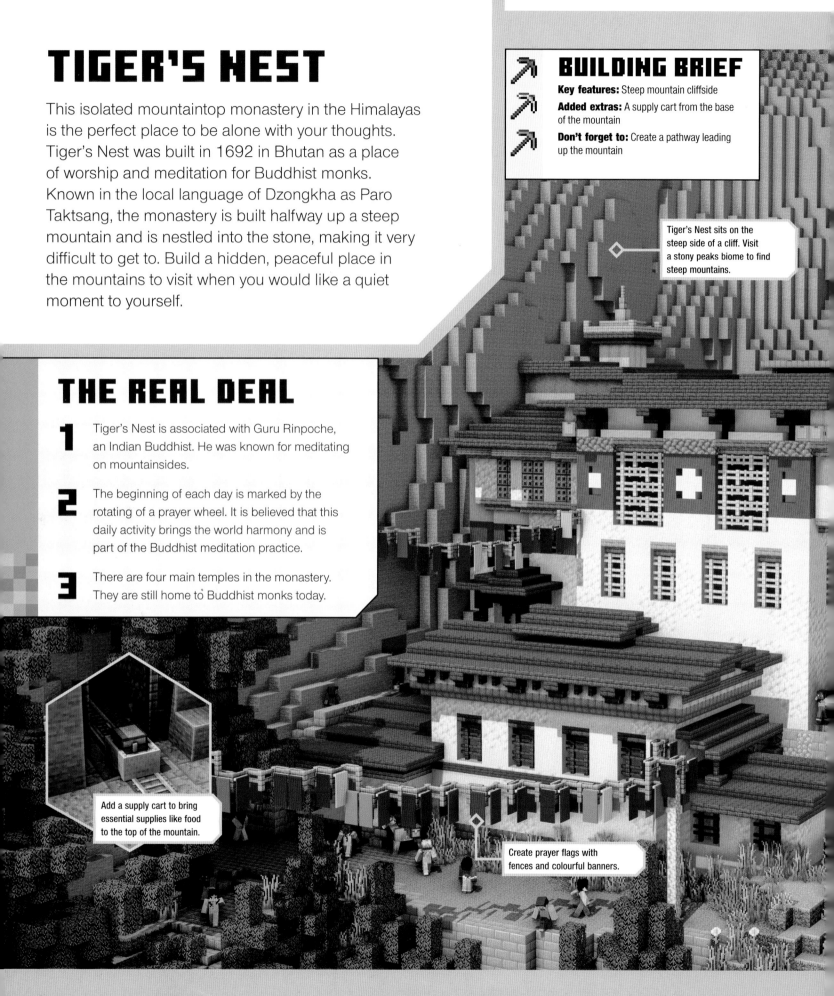

Tiger's Nest sits on the steep side of a cliff. Visit a stony peaks biome to find steep mountains.

THE REAL DEAL

1 Tiger's Nest is associated with Guru Rinpoche, an Indian Buddhist. He was known for meditating on mountainsides.

2 The beginning of each day is marked by the rotating of a prayer wheel. It is believed that this daily activity brings the world harmony and is part of the Buddhist meditation practice.

3 There are four main temples in the monastery. They are still home to Buddhist monks today.

Add a supply cart to bring essential supplies like food to the top of the mountain.

Create prayer flags with fences and colourful banners.

Use a combination of bamboo and birch wood to give the golden roofs a worn feel.

PRAYER FLAGS

The colourful banners hanging throughout this build are inspired by prayer flags. It is believed that the real flags send prayers when fluttering in the wind. Once crafted, banners can be placed on any block to ripple in the breeze. You can create bunting by hanging banners off fences or chains.

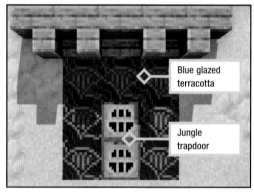

Blue glazed terracotta

Jungle trapdoor

UNIQUE PATTERNS

Glazed terracotta blocks are some of the most decorative blocks in Minecraft. They can be rotated when placing them down to make unique designs, like these colourful wall features. You can create glazed terracotta by smelting any dyed terracotta block.

The monastery walls are full of small details. Keep your builds coordinated by choosing the blocks you use carefully. For example, when building wooden features, use blocks with similar colours to the rest of the section. The mangrove wood really pops next to the Nether brick walls and red terracotta.

LOOK CLOSER

BEST BLOCKS

This Buddhist monastery is built in a traditional style, with white walls and golden roofs. It uses white concrete powder and calcite to give the walls a realistic grainy texture.

CALCITE

WHITE CONCRETE POWDER

AL-KHAZNEH, PETRA

Petra is an ancient desert city in present-day Jordan, and was the capital of the Nabataean Kingdom more than 2,000 years ago. It is famous for its many amazing buildings carved directly into rock, like this one, a royal tomb called al-Khazneh, or "The Treasury". Although Petra was well known to locals, it was "discovered" by Europeans in 1812. Build your own version of a carved city in Minecraft. A badlands biome would be an ideal location.

BUILDING BRIEF

Key features: Façade projecting from rock, 12 columns, carved details

Added extras: Hidden rooms

Don't forget to: Add a camel and some secret tunnels!

In architecture, the fancy "crown" at the top of a column is called a capital.

Mud bricks, slabs, and stairs create a textured effect alongside the brown terracotta.

BEST BLOCKS

The badlands are a great location for this model as you'll find lots of mountains and canyons, into which you can build your carved city into. Badlands are one of the rarest biomes in Minecraft, so it might take a while to find one. Use mud blocks and terracotta blocks to blend your build in with the surroundings.

MUD BRICK

TERRACOTTA

THE REAL DEAL

1 Petra thrived for centuries as a trade centre. Merchants crossed the desert to trade spices between the cities of Babylon and Damascus.

2 Petra was one of the wealthiest cities in the world for almost 900 years until it was badly damaged by earthquakes. It was abandoned in 663 CE.

3 Surrounded by mountains, Petra can only be reached by a small canyon called Al Siq, which is why it remained hidden to much of the world for more than 1,000 years.

ANCIENT DETAILS

Columns and pillars are essential for ancient builds, but you can add them to any model. They will make walls pop out and make a structure seem bigger. Add decorative details to the top of yours to make them look grander. These details are made from jungle fence gates and trapdoors.

Roam through a nearby badlands biome to find a canyon deep enough to hide the entrance to your city.

Add projecting details like this mud brick with spruce fence gates.

You don't have to build a huge model to recreate a big idea. Here, Petra is represented by a columned entrance that leads into the mountain. It could be part of a carved city or a house, or a hidden treasure trove could be inside.

TOP TIP

CREATING TEXTURE

Petra was carved into sandstone mountains, and you could easily recreate that in a Minecraft desert biome. However, this build uses terracotta from the badlands combined with mud block variants. Using lots of different blocks is a great way of adding texture and detail to your Minecraft builds.

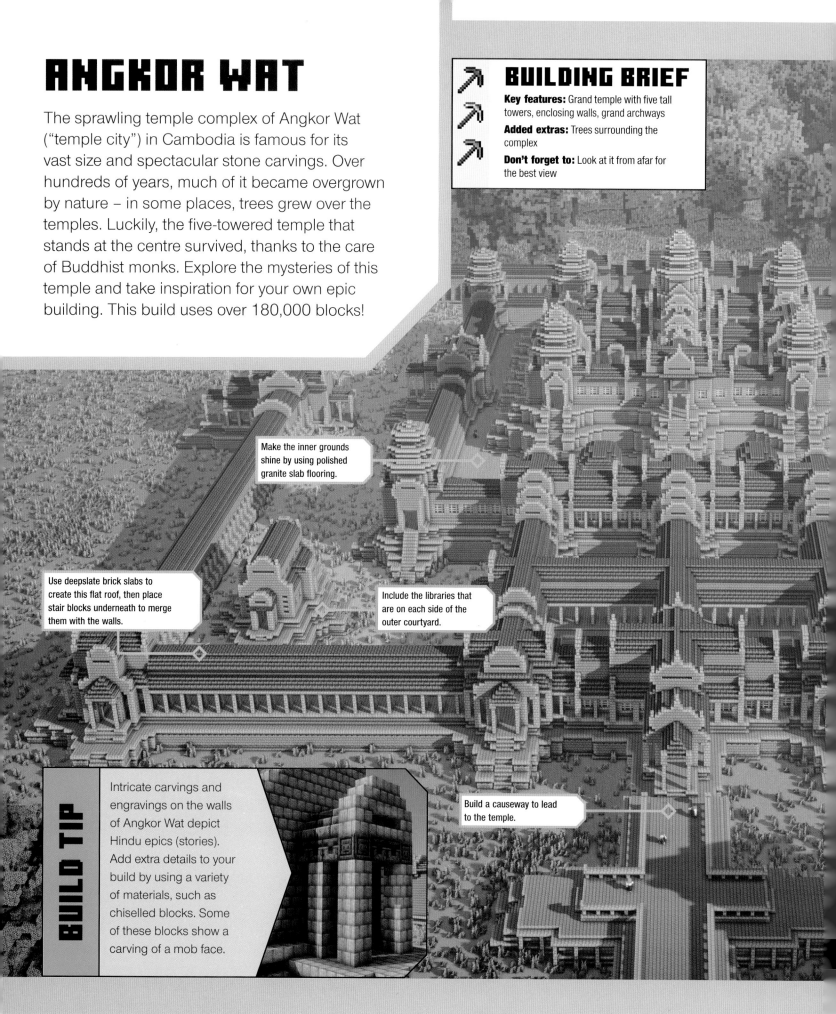

ANGKOR WAT

The sprawling temple complex of Angkor Wat ("temple city") in Cambodia is famous for its vast size and spectacular stone carvings. Over hundreds of years, much of it became overgrown by nature – in some places, trees grew over the temples. Luckily, the five-towered temple that stands at the centre survived, thanks to the care of Buddhist monks. Explore the mysteries of this temple and take inspiration for your own epic building. This build uses over 180,000 blocks!

BUILDING BRIEF

Key features: Grand temple with five tall towers, enclosing walls, grand archways

Added extras: Trees surrounding the complex

Don't forget to: Look at it from afar for the best view

Make the inner grounds shine by using polished granite slab flooring.

Use deepslate brick slabs to create this flat roof, then place stair blocks underneath to merge them with the walls.

Include the libraries that are on each side of the outer courtyard.

Build a causeway to lead to the temple.

BUILD TIP

Intricate carvings and engravings on the walls of Angkor Wat depict Hindu epics (stories). Add extra details to your build by using a variety of materials, such as chiselled blocks. Some of these blocks show a carving of a mob face.

THE REAL DEAL

1 The temple was built in the 12th century and is the largest religious monument in the world.

2 It was built to mimic the mythical mountain of Meru – the five towers reflect its five peaks.

3 The temple lines up with the points of a compass, with the main entrance pointing west. During the spring and autumn equinox (when day and night are equal length), the sun rises directly behind the central tower.

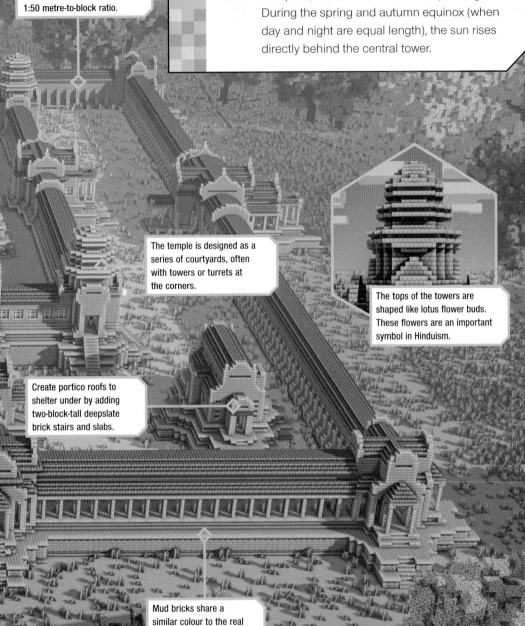

This Minecraft build has a 1:50 metre-to-block ratio.

The temple is designed as a series of courtyards, often with towers or turrets at the corners.

The tops of the towers are shaped like lotus flower buds. These flowers are an important symbol in Hinduism.

Create portico roofs to shelter under by adding two-block-tall deepslate brick stairs and slabs.

Mud bricks share a similar colour to the real Angkor Wat's sandstone.

TEXTURED TIERS

Every structure in Angkor Wat is incredibly detailed. This is recreated in Minecraft by adding tiers and tiers of texture using a mix of mud brick stairs, slabs, and walls. Start with a large base and build upwards, getting narrower as you reach the top. Use the stairs, slabs, and walls to create lots of sharp edges.

ARCHWAYS

Angkor Wat has a series of archways known as porticos. These go in every direction and provide shelter from the sun and rain. As with the rest of the Minecraft version, mud brick variants are the key building block for these corridors. The six-block-tall archways also include jungle fences for windows and dripstone blocks for columns.

BEST BLOCKS

This build recreates the shades of Angkor Wat. It is primarily built out of mud brick variants, with deepslate brick variants for roofing and dripstone blocks for the interiors.

DRIPSTONE

DEEPSLATE

MUD BRICKS

EIFFEL TOWER

The Eiffel Tower in Paris, France, is one of the most iconic landmarks in the world. Nicknamed the Iron Lady, the latticed iron structure stands high above the city, at 330 m (1,083 ft) tall. It was finished in 1889 to mark the centenary of the French Revolution. This Minecraft build is created using mostly mud blocks, to match the brown colour of the Eiffel Tower today. However, in the past the tower has been painted other colours, such as red. For a more colourful tower, try mangrove in your build, which is a deep red and has lots of useful variants.

BUILD TIP

When planning your build, start by creating a simple skeleton outline of your tower. Then, once you're happy with how it looks, prepare your favourite blocks and start filling out the details. If you're playing Survival mode, use lots of scaffolding to make sure you don't fall!

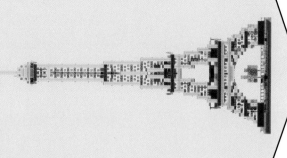

Make your third floor 70 blocks (274 m/900 ft) above the ground.

THE REAL DEAL

1 The Eiffel Tower is made from more than 18,000 pieces of iron, held together by more than 2.5 million rivets.

2 There are 1,665 steps to the top. These days there are lifts to help visitors reach the top, but the first visitors in 1889 just had to walk.

3 The top of the tower sways in the wind, bending by up to 7 cm (3 in). The metal shrinks when the weather is cold and expands when it's hot.

The Eiffel Tower has three levels. In the real tower, each level has a separate lift that can each carry around 1,700 visitors every hour.

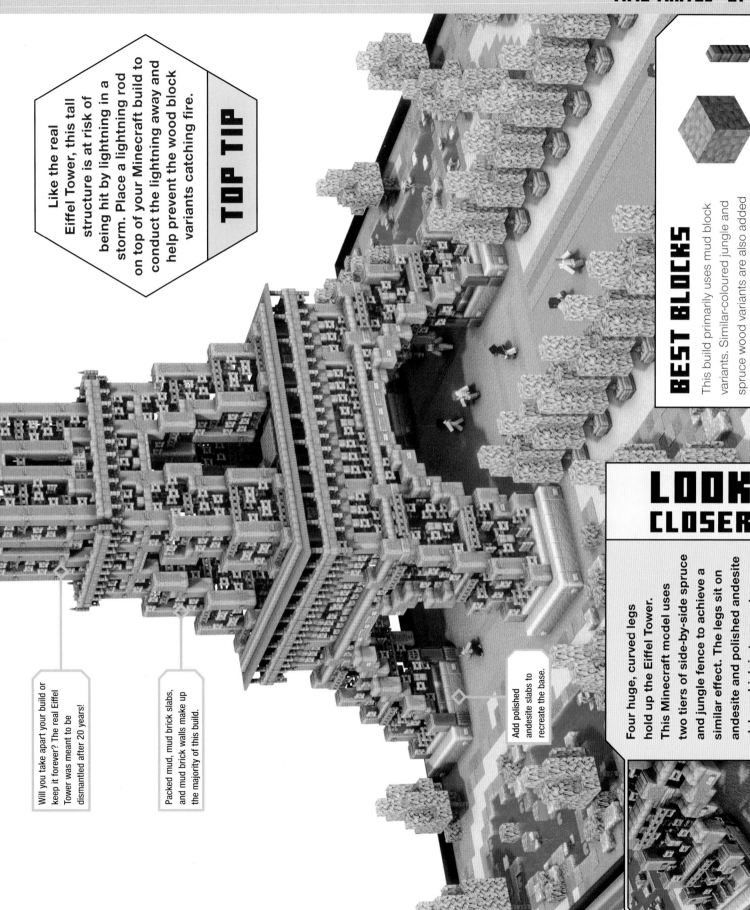

TOP TIP

Like the real Eiffel Tower, this tall structure is at risk of being hit by lightning in a storm. Place a lightning rod on top of your Minecraft build to conduct the lightning away and help prevent the wood block variants catching fire.

BEST BLOCKS

This build primarily uses mud block variants. Similar-coloured jungle and spruce wood variants are also added to make each of its features stand out and to add depth to the build.

LOOK CLOSER

Four huge, curved legs hold up the Eiffel Tower. This Minecraft model uses two tiers of side-by-side spruce and jungle fence to achieve a similar effect. The legs sit on andesite and polished andesite slabs, which in turn rest on a flat, solid andesite base.

Add polished andesite slabs to recreate the base.

Will you take apart your build or keep it forever? The real Eiffel Tower was meant to be dismantled after 20 years!

Packed mud, mud brick slabs, and mud brick walls make up the majority of this build.

PALAEONTOLOGY DIG SITE

Millions of years ago dinosaurs roamed the Earth. Thanks to the hard work of palaeontologists (scientists who study the remains of animals that lived millions of years ago) we know about more than 700 species of dinosaurs. They can be found anywhere in the world, even Antarctica. In Minecraft, you can find fossils in desert, swamp, and mangrove biomes, but why not build your own wherever you like?

BUILDING BRIEF

Key features: Dinosaur skeleton

Added extras: Field tents, site zoning grid, truck

Don't forget to: Research the dinosaur poses you could recreate in fossil form

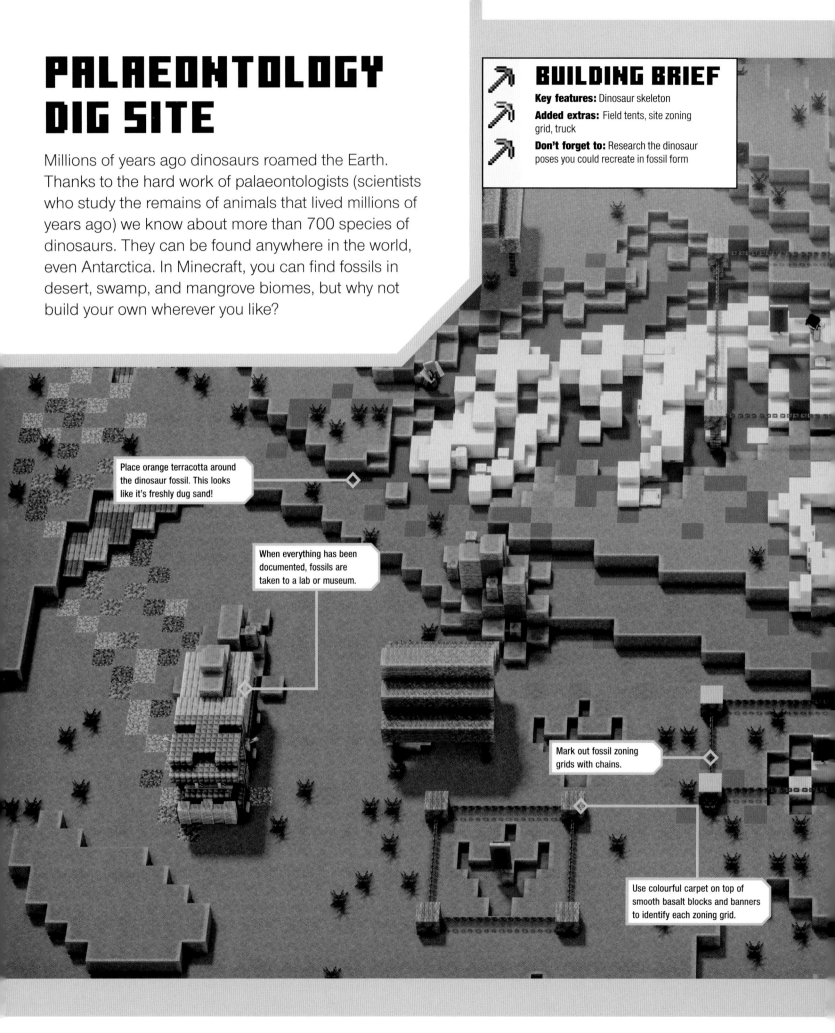

Place orange terracotta around the dinosaur fossil. This looks like it's freshly dug sand!

When everything has been documented, fossils are taken to a lab or museum.

Mark out fossil zoning grids with chains.

Use colourful carpet on top of smooth basalt blocks and banners to identify each zoning grid.

THE REAL DEAL

1 Fossils are the remains of animals and plants, such as bones, shells, feathers, and leaves, which are preserved in rock over thousands or millions of years.

2 The first descriptions of dinosaur fossils were made around 200 years ago. In 1824, the bones of a "great lizard" were given the scientific name *Megalosaurus*.

3 In China, rapid urban development is turning up lots of old ground, and with it, thousands of dinosaur fossils.

Complete dinosaur skeletons are extremely rare.

ZONING GRIDS

It's important that palaeontologists know exactly what fossils have been found and where. Coloured zoning grids help researchers map out the area and keep accurate notes. In your build, you could use dye and a loom to create numbered banners.

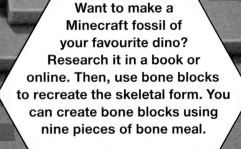

Want to make a Minecraft fossil of your favourite dino? Research it in a book or online. Then, use bone blocks to recreate the skeletal form. You can create bone blocks using nine pieces of bone meal.

TOP TIP

FIELD TENTS

In the real world, uncovering fossils can expose them to damaging sunlight and rain, so dig sites use field tents to protect the fossils. Build simple tent structures with wood fences, moss blocks, and wool to make your dig site look even more realistic.

BEST BLOCKS

Archaeology sites are temporary structures that are taken down after a dig is complete. Give your Minecraft dig site the same feel by using blocks that can be easily removed. Wool and wood are ideal for this because in Survival mode they can be moved quickly using shears and axes.

WOOD PLANKS

WOOL

WORLD HOUSES

Building a home is often the first project in a new Minecraft world, and the real world is just the same! Everywhere you go on our planet you will find unique and creative homes built from the resources in the local area. Let's explore a variety of traditional houses from around the world – and see how you can build them in Minecraft.

BUILDING BRIEF

Key features: Homes made out of locally sourced blocks and materials

Added extras: Tools and farms that reflect local lifestyles and environments

Don't forget to: Add doors and windows!

Use ladders to copy the wooden thatch bindings on the roof.

Place hay bales in a narrowing zig-zag pattern to create a conical-shaped roof.

Walls are made using stone-type blocks, such as cobblestone, andesite, and, of course, stone bricks.

Keep your water source from overflowing with dark oak trapdoors.

PALLOZA

A palloza is a traditional thatched house found in Galicia, Spain. Its walls were often made of stone, and the roof from straw and wood. There are few windows or openings to keep out the area's harsh winter winds.

FARMING

Farming was important to the people who lived in pallozas – their cows even lived in the house with them! Add farmland and water to your build to grow crops, and a cow for milk. Plant seeds to grow wheat for the cows and to craft hay bales for the roof.

BEST BLOCKS

This Minecraft recreation of a palloza has many similarities to the real-world version. It uses stone bricks for the walls, hay bales for the roof, and ladders to look like the wooden bindings.

STONE BRICKS

HAY BALES

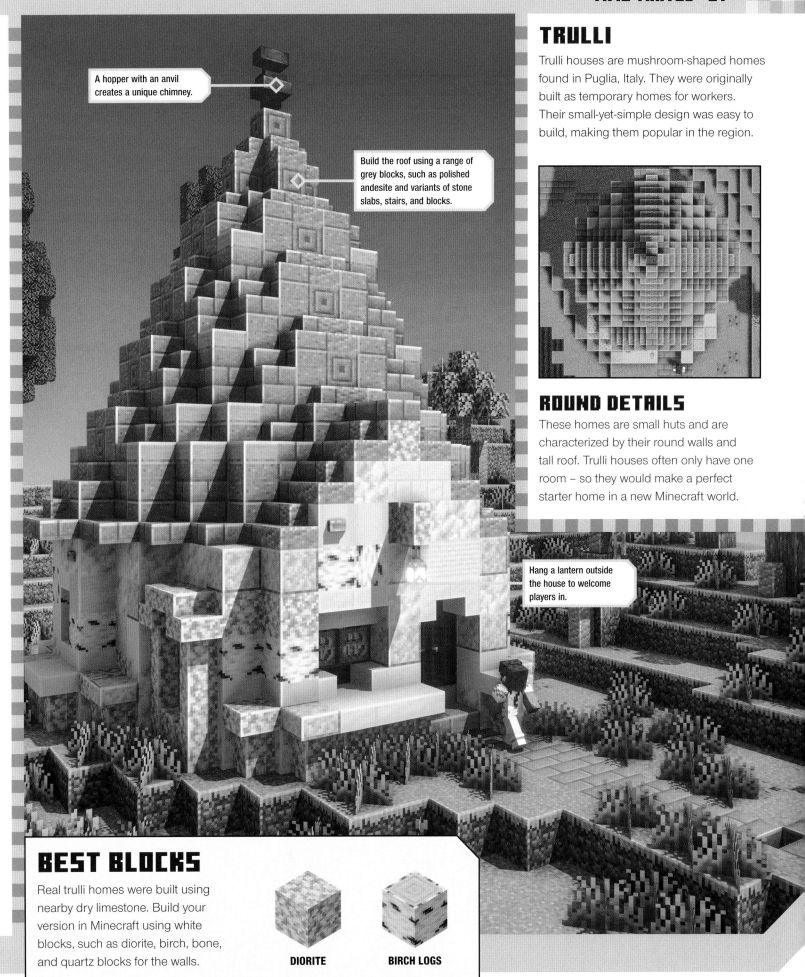

A hopper with an anvil creates a unique chimney.

Build the roof using a range of grey blocks, such as polished andesite and variants of stone slabs, stairs, and blocks.

TRULLI

Trulli houses are mushroom-shaped homes found in Puglia, Italy. They were originally built as temporary homes for workers. Their small-yet-simple design was easy to build, making them popular in the region.

ROUND DETAILS

These homes are small huts and are characterized by their round walls and tall roof. Trulli houses often only have one room – so they would make a perfect starter home in a new Minecraft world.

Hang a lantern outside the house to welcome players in.

BEST BLOCKS

Real trulli homes were built using nearby dry limestone. Build your version in Minecraft using white blocks, such as diorite, birch, bone, and quartz blocks for the walls.

DIORITE

BIRCH LOGS

THE REAL DEAL

Snow is a good insulator. The temperature in the Arctic can drop to a bone-chilling –45°C (–49°F), while inside an igloo it could be a milder –7°C (–19°F).

INUIT IGLOO

Igloos are shelters made of snow that are traditionally used by the Inuit people of the Arctic region. Igloos are an important part of the Inuit culture, and provide shelter from the extreme cold and windy weather.

INTERIOR

The inside of a real igloo is kept warm with animal furs and a stove. In Minecraft, you don't need to worry about the cold, but you can still make your igloo nice and cosy with carpets, banners, and a warm campfire.

Inside, a real igloo can fit up to five people!

Add an entrance tunnel to the igloo. The entrances are small to help prevent cold air from entering.

Inuit sleds are made from salvaged wood. This stationary sled has slabs, stairs, signs, a fence gate – and a tame wolf!

Create a hole in the ice to cast your fishing line through.

BEST BLOCKS

To build igloos, the Inuit make use of the most widely available resource in the Arctic – snow! Similarly, this build uses snow blocks to recreate the dome-shaped structure. Inside, carpets and banners replace the furs.

SNOW BLOCK

RED CARPET

TONGKONAN

Tongkonan are the traditional homes of the Toraja people in Indonesia. It is thought that the houses' distinctive boat-shaped roofs are to remind the Toraja of the boats that were used to first sail to the islands.

Build a spruce staircase with trapdoor banisters to access the main room.

Use birch fence gates and a birch fence to recreate the front roof beams on the building.

UNIQUE ROOF

The unusual roofs of these houses take the Torajan a long time to build with lots of layered wood. Replicate this in Minecraft by using all kinds of wood variants including acacia logs and spruce slabs.

Use dark oak fences to create pillars outside the house.

Add piles (or stilts) made from oak wood. These piles keep real tongkonans safe from flooding.

BEST BLOCKS

The Torajan used locally available materials, which they painted in bright colours. Use colourful wood, such as dark oak and acacia planks, to recreate the painted look or create a plain coloured one with bamboo blocks.

ACACIA PLANKS

DARK OAK PLANKS

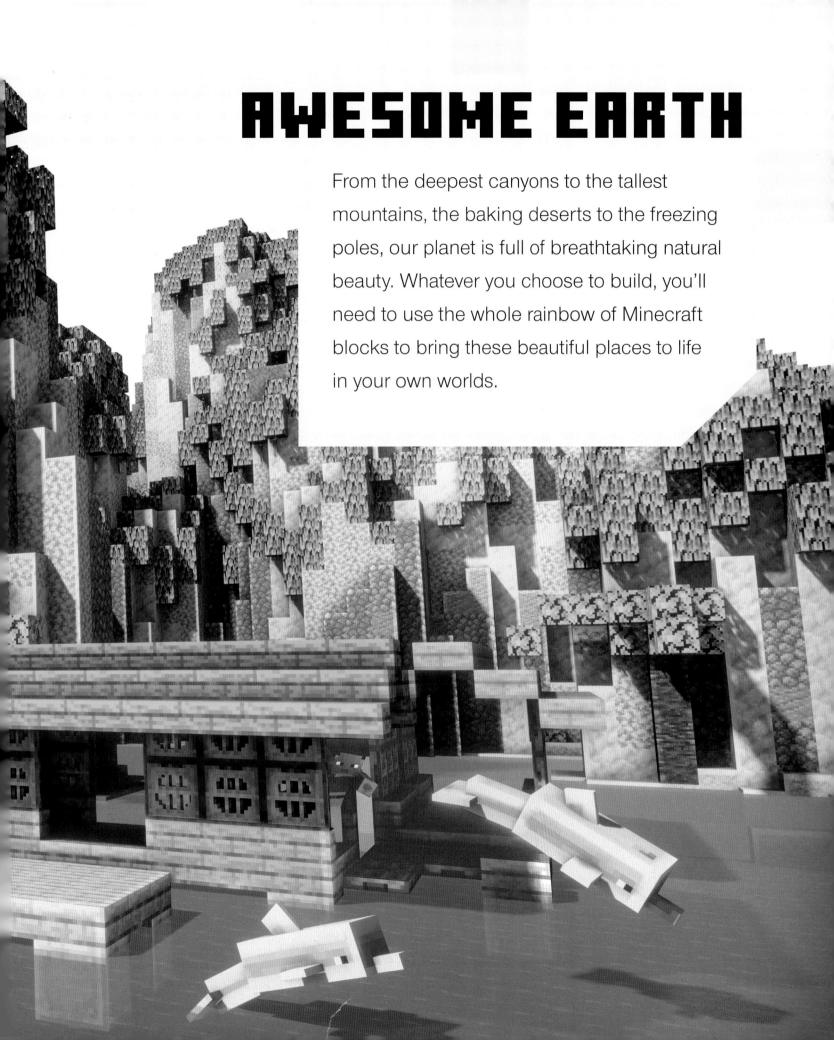

AWESOME EARTH

From the deepest canyons to the tallest mountains, the baking deserts to the freezing poles, our planet is full of breathtaking natural beauty. Whatever you choose to build, you'll need to use the whole rainbow of Minecraft blocks to bring these beautiful places to life in your own worlds.

MOUNT EVEREST BASE CAMP

Climbing Mount Everest, the world's tallest mountain, is incredibly dangerous. Before even attempting to scale it, climbers have to spend a few days at base camp getting used to being so high up. Climbing in Survival mode can be pretty dangerous too, so start by enchanting your boots with Feather Falling to save you from respawning back home. Then, build a base camp to rest in. You could make it so great that you won't want to bother climbing the mountain!

BUILDING BRIEF

Key features: Tents and other temporary structures

Added extras: Outdoor lighting to deter hostile mobs

Don't forget to: Pack lots of supply crates

CHANGE IT!

Many Everest climbers wish there were more comforts and services available at base camp. What non-essential features could you add in Minecraft? How about a skating rink, a gym, or a cosy cinema?

Use shulker boxes to transport supplies.

It's important to stay warm in the Himalayas. Build structures like this to keep the cold out.

Add outdoor lanterns to keep the camp safe and prevent hostile mobs from spawning at night.

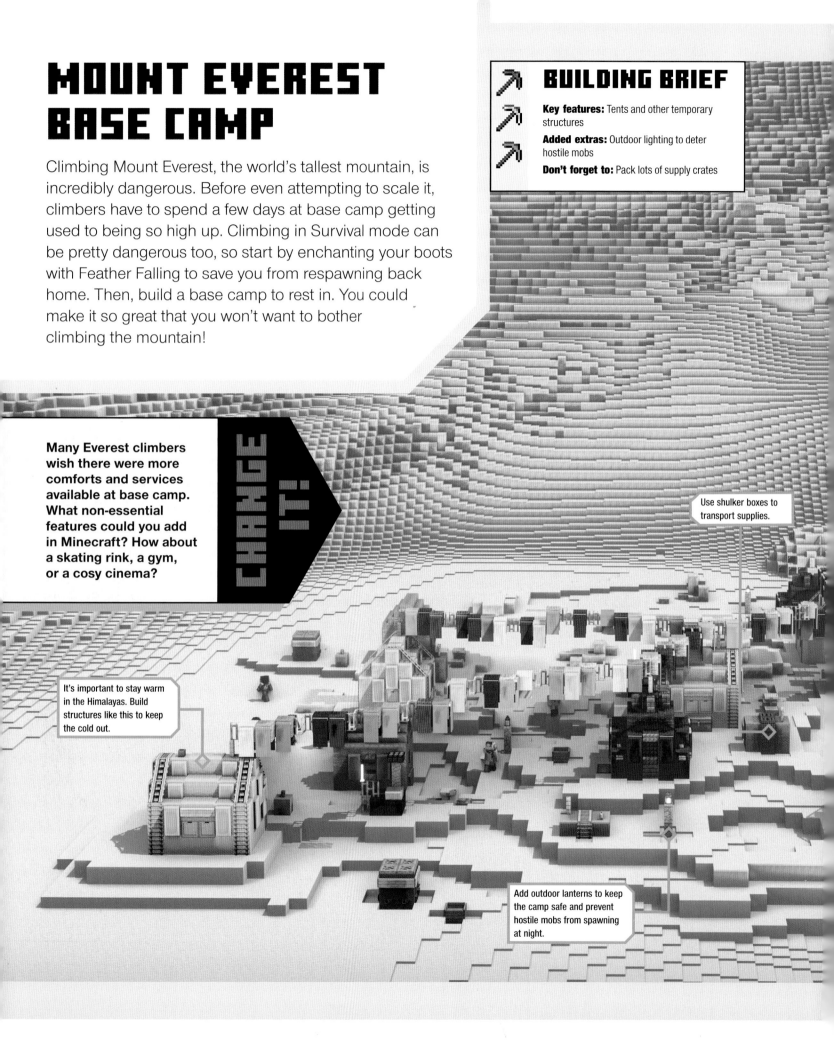

THE REAL DEAL

1 Mount Everest in the Himalaya mountain range is the tallest peak in the world at 8,849 m (29,032 ft) high.

2 However, Mount Everest is getting taller. It sits on two continental plates that push it an extra 4 mm (0.157 in) higher each year.

3 To be allowed to climb Mount Everest, climbers must be fit, healthy, and have already climbed a nearby 6,500-m- (21,300-ft-) high mountain.

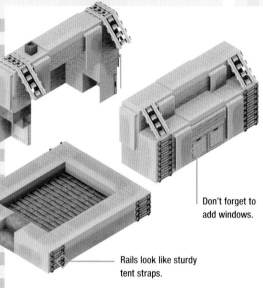

Don't forget to add windows.

Rails look like sturdy tent straps.

Falling into powder snow can cause freezing damage. Equip yourself with leather boots to walk around safely.

Use red sandstone and coloured concrete to make temporary structures.

Anchor your tents securely against the fierce winds, using rails and ladders.

LIVING QUARTERS

Climbers stay at base camp for three to five days in temporary shelters. These shelters are sturdy tents that need to be firmly anchored to the ground. You can create warm shelters in Minecraft using yellow wool, banners, and concrete. This build uses ladders and rails to recreate the anchoring, and trapdoors for windows.

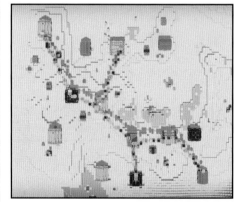

CAMP PLANNING

You can only climb Mount Everest during the summer trekking season, so no one uses the real base camp during winter months and it is rebuilt each year. You can either dismantle your Minecraft build and start again or just give it a spring renovation. What can you improve on to make it more comfortable? What new structures might you add?

BEST BLOCKS

To keep the area tidy for other climbers, use easily removable blocks such as wool and wood. Use durable blocks, like concrete and red sandstone, to copy the safer materials used in camp kitchens.

RED SANDSTONE

YELLOW CONCRETE

RAINBOW LAKE

Yellowstone National Park in the USA sits over a supervolcano that last erupted about 150,000 years ago. Volcanic activity has created a spectacular landscape with more than 10,000 hot springs. One of Yellowstone's most striking natural wonders is Rainbow Lake. This multi-coloured lake sits in the Yellowstone Caldera, a crater left behind after the supervolcano's last eruption. It gets its colours from the heat-loving bacteria that live there. You can recreate this stunning lake using the many colourful blocks Minecraft has to offer.

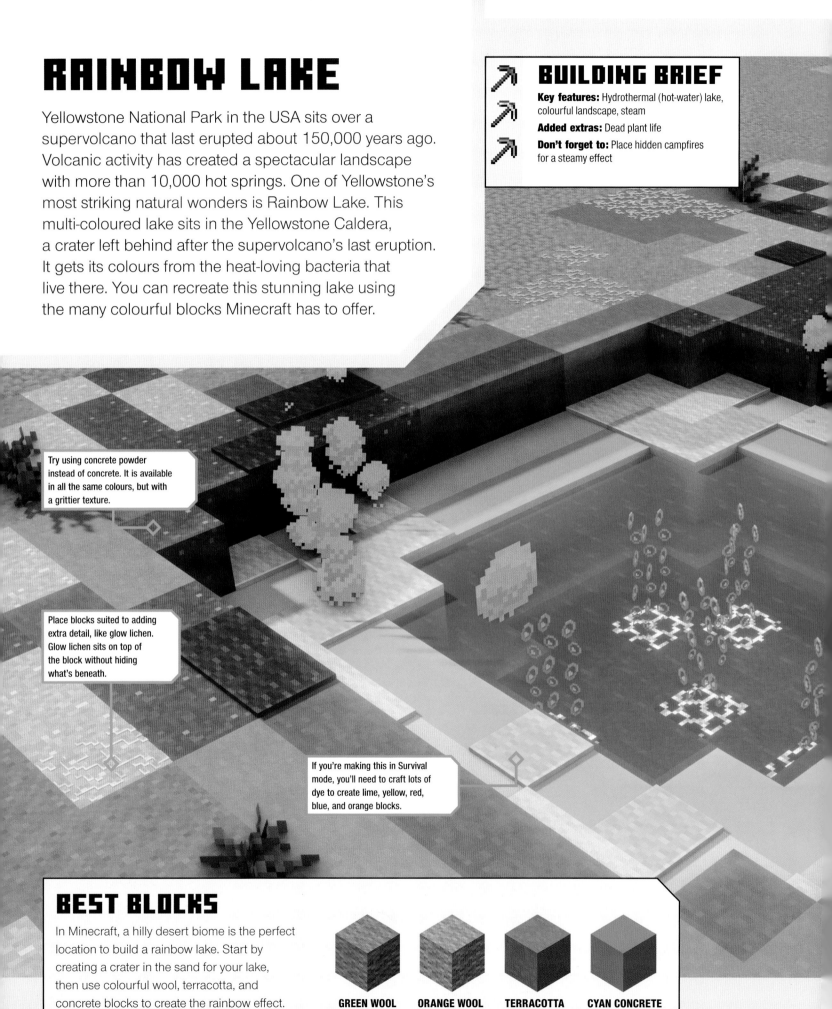

BUILDING BRIEF

Key features: Hydrothermal (hot-water) lake, colourful landscape, steam

Added extras: Dead plant life

Don't forget to: Place hidden campfires for a steamy effect

Try using concrete powder instead of concrete. It is available in all the same colours, but with a grittier texture.

Place blocks suited to adding extra detail, like glow lichen. Glow lichen sits on top of the block without hiding what's beneath.

If you're making this in Survival mode, you'll need to craft lots of dye to create lime, yellow, red, blue, and orange blocks.

BEST BLOCKS

In Minecraft, a hilly desert biome is the perfect location to build a rainbow lake. Start by creating a crater in the sand for your lake, then use colourful wool, terracotta, and concrete blocks to create the rainbow effect.

GREEN WOOL   **ORANGE WOOL**   **TERRACOTTA**   **CYAN CONCRETE**

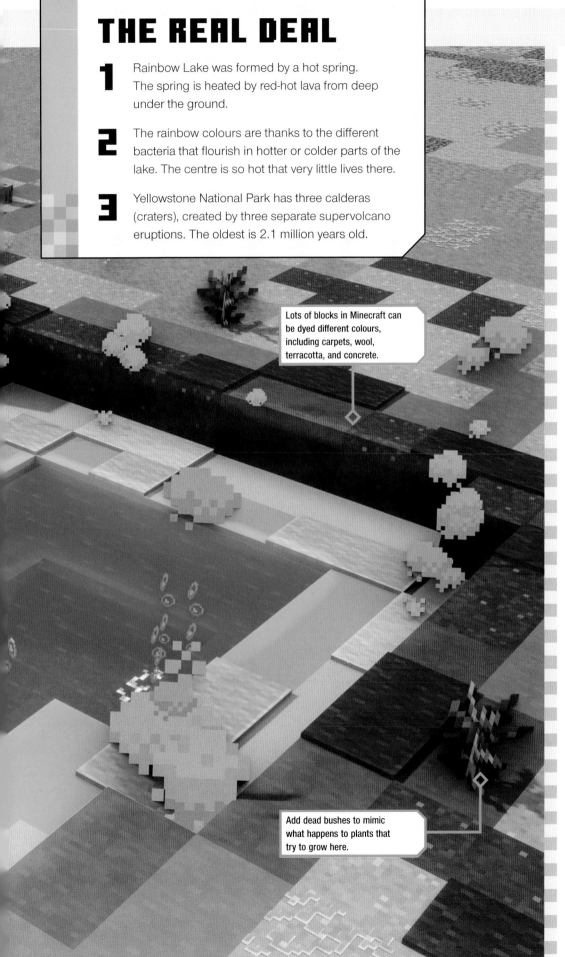

THE REAL DEAL

1 Rainbow Lake was formed by a hot spring. The spring is heated by red-hot lava from deep under the ground.

2 The rainbow colours are thanks to the different bacteria that flourish in hotter or colder parts of the lake. The centre is so hot that very little lives there.

3 Yellowstone National Park has three calderas (craters), created by three separate supervolcano eruptions. The oldest is 2.1 million years old.

Lots of blocks in Minecraft can be dyed different colours, including carpets, wool, terracotta, and concrete.

Add dead bushes to mimic what happens to plants that try to grow here.

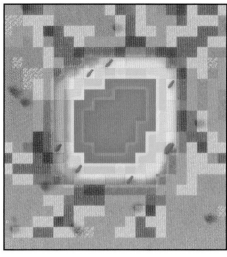

CREATING TEXTURE

If you take a closer look, this build is not flat. The surface is slightly uneven to represent the natural, weathered look of Rainbow Lake. To achieve this effect, you can just place carpets on matching colour blocks. This will raise the ground slightly, adding an impressive realistic detail to the finished build.

Carpet

Campfire

STEAM EFFECT

Here's a clever trick to create the steam of a hot spring in Minecraft. Simply place campfires among the blocks and then hide them with similar-coloured carpets. The smoke travels through the carpet, but the campfire is hidden beneath.

TROPICAL RAINFOREST

Tropical rainforests cover less than three percent of the Earth, yet these lush environments are home to at least half of all the world's plants and animals, which makes them fascinating and important places. They are found near the equator (an imaginary line that runs around the middle of the Earth), where it is warm and wet. In Minecraft, you can not only explore the rainforest depths, search for exotic animals, and gather rare resources, but also have a blast planting and nurturing new rainforests!

BUILDING BRIEF

Key features: Custom-made trees, canopy bridge, treehouse (see more on p72–73)

Added extras: Exotic plants and mobs

Don't forget to: Add a natural feel with long vines

Wildlife such as parrots and ocelots will thrive in your rainforest.

Build a wooden bridge to connect two peaks.

Use tuff to create the appearance of weathered stone.

LOOK CLOSER

As some of the most diverse places on Earth, rainforests are full of amazing tropical plants. Fill your Minecraft rainforest with colourful plants, such as this hanging spore blossom. This build uses spruce fences to attach the blossoms to the trees.

THE REAL DEAL

1 Rainforests provide a home to over 1,500 different species of birds, 300 species of mammals, and 2.5 million species of insects.

2 This environment receives an average of 2,000 mm (80 in) of rain every year, making it one of the wettest ecosystems on Earth.

3 Rainforests are the lungs of the planet, producing 20 percent of the oxygen humans and animals need to breathe.

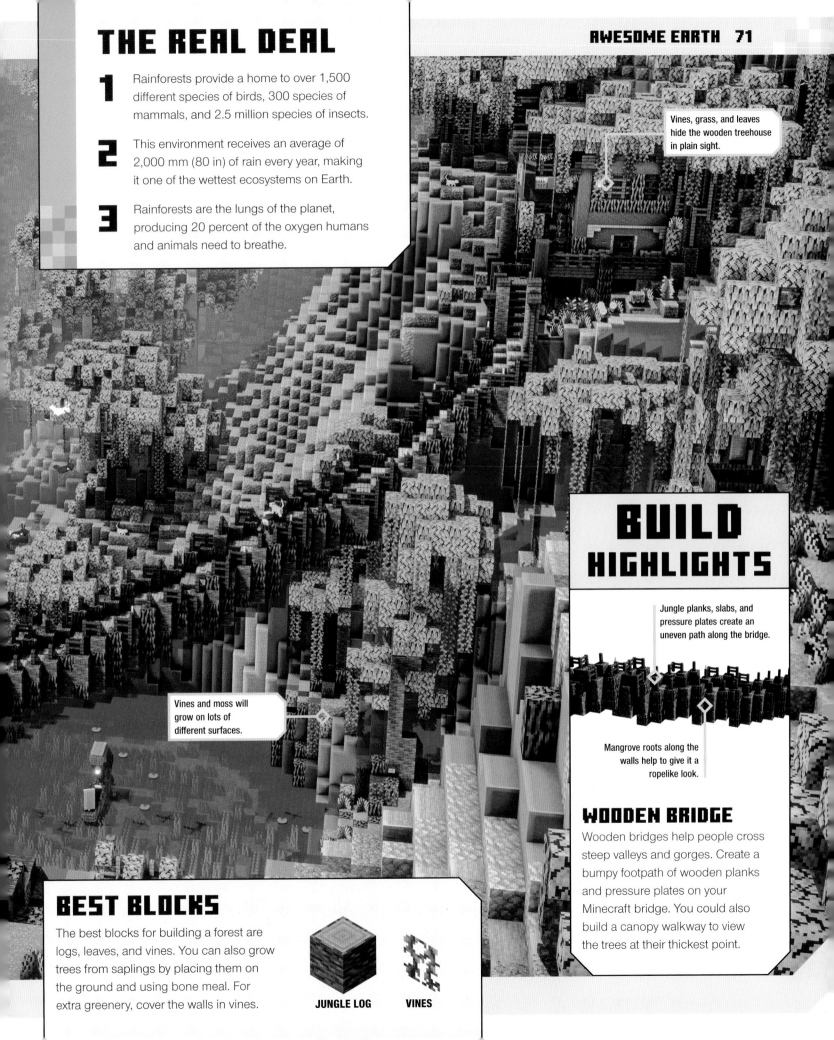

Vines, grass, and leaves hide the wooden treehouse in plain sight.

Vines and moss will grow on lots of different surfaces.

BUILD HIGHLIGHTS

Jungle planks, slabs, and pressure plates create an uneven path along the bridge.

Mangrove roots along the walls help to give it a ropelike look.

WOODEN BRIDGE

Wooden bridges help people cross steep valleys and gorges. Create a bumpy footpath of wooden planks and pressure plates on your Minecraft bridge. You could also build a canopy walkway to view the trees at their thickest point.

BEST BLOCKS

The best blocks for building a forest are logs, leaves, and vines. You can also grow trees from saplings by placing them on the ground and using bone meal. For extra greenery, cover the walls in vines.

JUNGLE LOG   **VINES**

TROPICAL RAINFOREST: IN FOCUS

Jungle biomes are among the most densely forested biomes in Minecraft. They are so full of jungle trees and bamboo that there's almost no space to walk around. The trees here grow extra tall. This makes them the perfect starting place to create your rainforest – and to build a hidden treehouse base, too!

RAINFOREST LAYERS

A real rainforest has four layers Each one provides a home for different plants and animals. Recreate these layers in Minecraft. Place lots of jungle tree leaves on the ground, and hang vines from all the trees.

EMERGENT LAYER

Build a few very tall trees that reach high into the sky.

JUNGLE MOBS

Just like real-world rainforests, Minecraft's jungles are home to unique creatures. Keep your eyes open for the parrots in the trees. On the ground, you might even find pandas munching on bamboo and ocelots sneaking up on chickens. Bring them to your own rainforest with spawn eggs.

CANOPY

The densest part of the rainforest is the leafy canopy, created by shorter trees. Use regular Minecraft trees to fill the area. Their short branches are thick with leaves.

UNDERSTOREY

Below the canopy is the understorey. Very little light breaks through the canopy so few plants grow here.

FOREST FLOOR

The floor receives almost no light at all. Place fallen leaves and ferns in your Minecraft version.

TREEHOUSE

Keep your treehouse safe from hostile mobs by hiding it deep in the rainforest. Disguise your base by using nearby blocks for building materials. This treehouse uses natural-looking dark oak blocks, packed mud, brown mushroom blocks, mangrove roots, and more.

KITCHEN

This kitchen is filled with the essentials for an explorer: a furnace, a crafting table, and a cartography table. Here you can cook food, smelt ores for equipment, and create maps.

Create the roof using dark oak slabs and stairs to blend into the jungle surroundings.

Add details to your treehouse with fences, buttons, trapdoors, stairs, and stripped wood.

BEDROOM

This cosy room is only six blocks long and five blocks wide. It has space for beds for two players. Add spruce fence windows and brown mushroom block and packed mud walls for a natural feel.

Build stilts using mangrove roots to raise your treehouse above the forest floor.

BUILD TIP

Try to use the existing forest terrain to shape your treehouse. Build outwards in each direction, shaping your base around the original trees. The tree trunks could even become part of the base's walls. If you want to add new trees, plant saplings and grow them with bone meal.

GREAT BARRIER REEF

Located in the Coral Sea off the coast of Queensland, Australia, the Great Barrier Reef is the world's largest living structure. Although coral can be mistaken for rocks, it is actually groups of tiny living creatures called polyps. Colourful plant-like algae live inside the coral, and lots of fish and marine life live around it. In this underwater Minecraft world you can build, explore, and discover many interesting creatures. So go get your turtle shell helmet and start building!

Coral clusters come in all shapes and sizes.

The reef's shallow waters and stormy weather make it a hazardous area for ships. Find an existing wreckage for your build, or make your own using oak and spruce variants.

Feed dolphins some raw cod or raw salmon and they'll bring you to buried treasure.

Pollution and climate change are making the ocean warmer and more acidic, which is causing problems for coral. The algae can no longer live on the coral and the coral turns white (bleaches). In Minecraft, if coral is placed outside water it turns into dead coral within moments.

LOOK CLOSER

THE REAL DEAL

1 A barrier reef is a long, narrow coral formation, mostly underwater, and usually located parallel to the shore.

2 It takes millions of years to form a coral reef. The coral polyps build hard protective cases around themselves, and these cases form large, rocklike reefs.

3 The Great Barrier Reef is 2,600 km (1,600 miles) long and can even be seen from space.

CORAL CLUSTERS

Corals need water to survive. In Minecraft, submerge the coral in water, or place it next to water or a waterlogged block to keep it alive. Corals generate in clusters of up to 5x5 blocks wide and 8 blocks tall. Or you can create them yourself in Creative mode. There are three types of coral: coral, coral blocks, and coral fans. Use coral blocks for the main structure and coral fans to add extra detail.

In Minecraft, sea pickles generate in clusters of up to four.

Your coral reef can provide homes for animals such as tropical fish, pufferfish, turtles, and dolphins.

NIGHT VISION

It's very dark at the bottom of the ocean due to the lack of sunlight, so you cannot see very far. Luckily, in Minecraft you can craft potions of Night Vision to help see what's going on around you underwater. Craft one using a water bottle, Nether wart, and a golden carrot in a brewing stand.

BEST BLOCKS

For a coral reef like this one, you'll need lots of corals and sand blocks. You can also add realistic details such as kelp and seaweed, or build a sunken shipwreck and treasure chest.

BRAIN CORAL

TUBE CORAL

VICTORIA FALLS

Victoria Falls is a vast waterfall located in the Zambezi River, on the borders of Zambia and Zimbabwe in Africa. It is known in Zambia as "Mosi-oa-Tunya", meaning "the smoke that thunders", due to its thunderous roar that can be heard from miles away and the mists that often surround it. To recreate this epic waterfall in Minecraft, find a ravine in a jungle biome. A waterfall will require lots and lots of water, so make sure you create an infinite water source before starting to build.

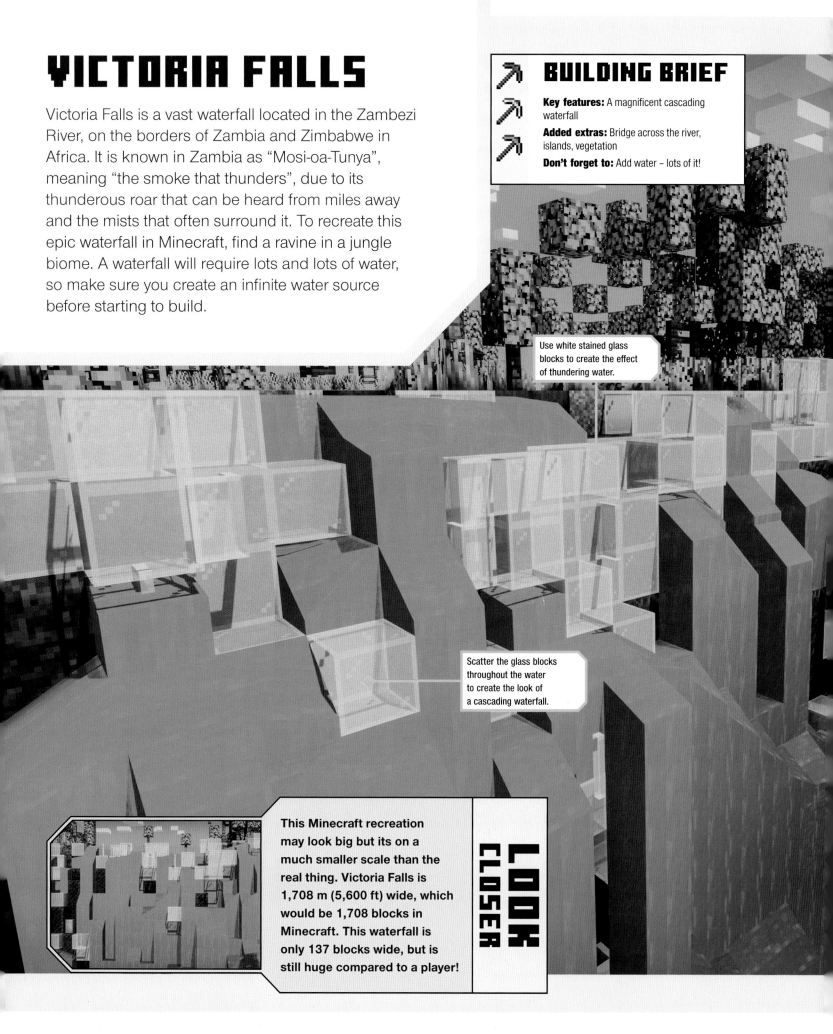

BUILDING BRIEF

Key features: A magnificent cascading waterfall

Added extras: Bridge across the river, islands, vegetation

Don't forget to: Add water – lots of it!

Use white stained glass blocks to create the effect of thundering water.

Scatter the glass blocks throughout the water to create the look of a cascading waterfall.

This Minecraft recreation may look big but its on a much smaller scale than the real thing. Victoria Falls is 1,708 m (5,600 ft) wide, which would be 1,708 blocks in Minecraft. This waterfall is only 137 blocks wide, but is still huge compared to a player!

LOOK CLOSER

THE REAL DEAL

1 The European name "Victoria Falls" is in honour of the British Queen Victoria. British explorer David Livingstone was the first European to visit Victoria Falls.

2 Victoria Falls is up to 1,708 m (5,604 ft) wide and 108.2 m (355 ft) high.

3 Victoria Falls is protected by the Mosi-oa-Tunya National Park on the Zambia side and the Victoria Falls National Park on the Zimbabwe side.

LOOK AT THE VIEW!

Knife Edge Bridge gives tourists a spectacular view of Victoria Falls. But it's only for those who like heights as the narrow bridge feels like standing on a knife's edge! This sturdier Minecraft bridge is made of stone bricks, dirt paths, and cobblestone. You can also use mossy block variants for extra detailing.

Add lots of trees and plants to recreate a fertile river bank.

Use coarse dirt, mud, and lots of variants of wood blocks for the solid ground behind the water.

Terraform a ravine from mangrove wood, mud, and muddy mangrove roots.

ISLANDS

Victoria Falls divides the Zambezi River into the Upper Zambezi (above the waterfall) and the Middle/Lower Zambezi at the bottom, and different species of fish flourish in these different parts. The Falls are also dotted with several small islands. Finding a ravine is a great way to get started on a build like this in Minecraft, or you can terraform your own. To add an island, collect a few stacks of dirt blocks and add them directly to the bottom of the river.

BEST BLOCKS

To create the "whitewater" look of a powerful waterfall use white coloured blocks such as white stained glass. Place them inside and outside the waterfall to create a splashy, moving water effect.

WHITE STAINED GLASS

CAÑO CRISTALES

The Caño Cristales river, also known as the "River of Five Colours", is a beautiful waterway in Colombia. For most of the year, this river is just like many others. But for a few months, when the water levels are at their shallowest, a rare aquatic plant transforms the river to a vibrant red. The red contrasts with the green waterweeds, yellow sand, and blue and black waters to create a dazzling liquid rainbow. Build a spectacular rainbow river in Minecraft, using colourful blocks instead of plants.

Make a waterfall from stone and cobblestone blocks for the river to flow over.

BUILDING BRIEF

Key features: Multicoloured riverbed, rocks, rapids, waterfalls

Added extras: The trees surrounding the river

Don't forget to: Remove the gravel and dirt blocks from the riverbed

The red *Macarenia* plant stands out against the other colours of the river.

Use cobwebs to give a white, foamy effect where the water crashes down at the bottom of waterfalls and to show it tumbling around rocky rapids. Another way to create this effect is by adding magma or soul sand under water source blocks to make bubble columns.

LOOK CLOSER

THE REAL DEAL

1 The rare, red *Macarenia clavigera* plant is a riverweed, and is found nowhere else on Earth.

2 The Caño Cristales river has many rapids and waterfalls. It has no fish because the water contains very little food.

3 The rainbow phenomenon occurs from around August to November every year.

RED COLOUR

The very rare *Macarenia clavigera* plant can't be found in Minecraft. But you can use red wool, mangrove planks, red terracotta, and netherrack instead.

CLEAR WATER

The Caño Cristales river is unusual in that it has no sediment or mud on its riverbed. The gravel and dirt have been removed from this Minecraft version too. The Minecraft river uses a variety of blocks, such as terracotta, concrete, and hay bales, so that it stays bright and colourful in daylight.

> Make sure the river is very shallow — this one is only two blocks deep at its deepest.

> Create the liquid rainbow effect with colourful lime concrete, cyan wool, red terracotta, hay bales, gold blocks, and more.

BEST BLOCKS

It's known as the "rainbow river" for a reason. More than 15 different blocks have been used to recreate the colours of the rainbow in this model.

RED WOOL

COBBLESTONE

NETHERRACK

CYAN WOOL

WET SPONGE

HAY BALE

GREEN WOOL

GOLD

TORRES DEL PAINE, PATAGONIA

The stunning Torres del Paine National Park in Patagonia, Chile, is a UNESCO World Biosphere Reserve, which is a designated learning place for sustainable development. Torres del Paine is known for its diverse landscapes, ranging from snow-capped mountains to emerald forests and azure lakes. Why not create your own national park in Minecraft? What biome will you choose? Will you have mountains? How will you make it visitor friendly? Grab your favourite blocks and start terraforming!

Create your own custom terrains, like these mountain peaks. Snow and snow layers are perfect for recreating the snowy look of Torres del Paine.

The park's mountains are famous for appearing blue from a distance. Add cyan terracotta to your build to give it a blue hue.

LOOK CLOSER

Bright lighting is not great for nocturnal wildlife – but in your Minecraft world, lighting is useful for walking around at night. Create subtle lighting using hidden light sources. These are torches hidden beneath grey carpets (fire won't spread from these in Minecraft).

Add colourful shrubs, such as flowering azalea to recreate the vegetation in Torres del Paine.

THE REAL DEAL

1 Torres del Paine was formed around 12 million years ago. The three tall granite towerlike peaks (*torres* means "towers in Spanish) formed when glaciers wore down layers of sedimentary rock.

2 The three granite mountains stand 1,500 m (4,900 ft) above sea level.

3 Torres del Paine is home to lots of unique wildlife, including guanacos (they're a bit like llamas) and birds, such as rheas and condors.

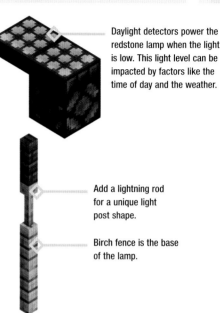

Daylight detectors power the redstone lamp when the light is low. This light level can be impacted by factors like the time of day and the weather.

Add a lightning rod for a unique light post shape.

Birch fence is the base of the lamp.

LIGHTING

These sensor lights are the perfect way to add an element of human civilization to your build, in a safe and eco-friendly way. In Survival mode they will also prevent hostile mobs from spawning. They're built using fences, a lightning rod, and a redstone lamp. Add daylight detectors to ensure they do not come on in the day.

Mimic the shape of tents with your eco lodges. Use rails to recreate the guy lines that hold them down.

ECO LODGE

National parks are protected spaces that allow nature to thrive, but they are also amazing places to visit. Environmentally friendly eco lodges are ideal places for visitors to stay in. They're built from sustainable materials and designed to blend in with nature. Build your eco lodge in Minecraft with natural resources, such as wood, mud, and grass.

Create shrubs with a varied shape using dead bushes with azalea leaves on top.

BEST BLOCKS

Building a nature reserve in Minecraft is all about using naturally occurring blocks. The landscape in this build is made using mossy cobblestone, cyan terracotta, tuff, and deepslate.

CYAN TERRACOTTA

DEEPSLATE

SUGAR LOAF MOUNTAIN

Sugar Loaf Mountain overlooks Rio de Janeiro in Brazil. It got its name from the stacks of sugar that were grown and exported from Brazil during the 19th century. Recreating this distinctive shape will be a great test for your Minecraft terraforming skills! Search for a mountainous landscape to get started. Use your favourite blocks to terraform Sugar Loaf mountain and smaller hills, and then build a cable car system to make climbing the mountain quick and easy.

THE REAL DEAL

1 Experts think that Sugar Loaf Mountain is more than 600 million years old. It formed underground before slowly emerging.

2 Sugar Loaf's cable car system carries more than a million tourists up the 395-m- (1,296-ft-) mountain every year!

3 The mountain is also popular with extreme rock climbers, and there are more than 270 different climbing routes for them to try.

Build cable car stations at the top, middle, and bottom of your mountain.

Plant trees and plants from the jungle biome to recreate the mountain's lush look.

Place bamboo shoots to grow bamboo or find it in jungle biomes, where it grows abundantly up to 16 blocks high.

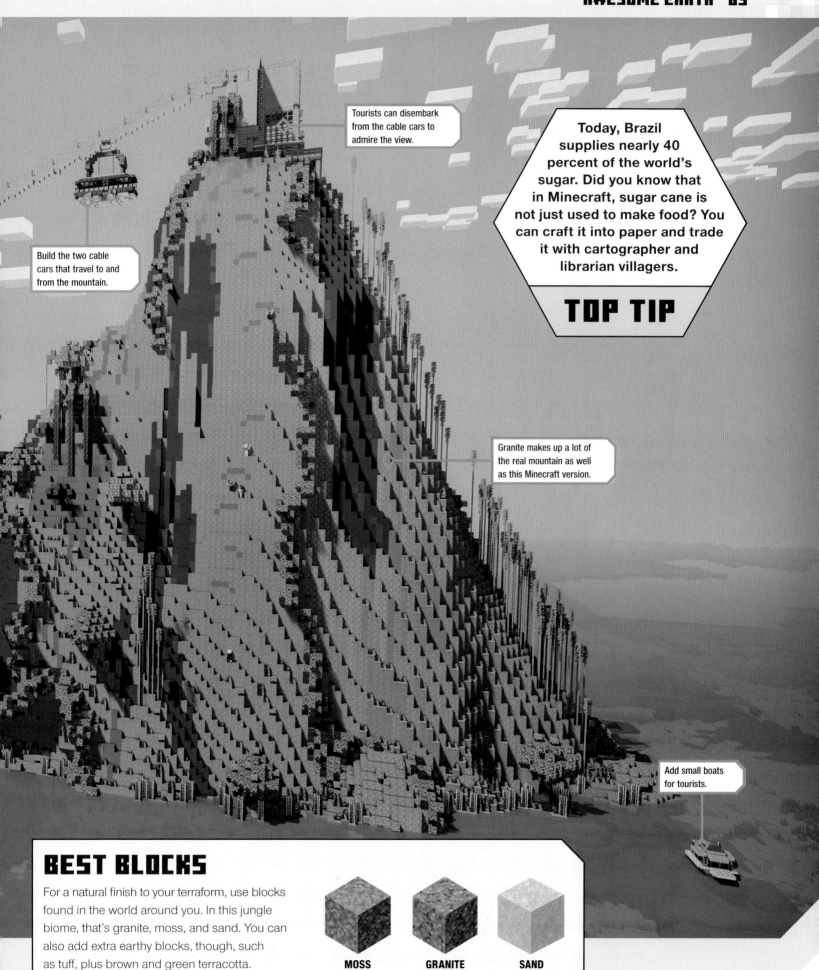

Tourists can disembark from the cable cars to admire the view.

Build the two cable cars that travel to and from the mountain.

Today, Brazil supplies nearly 40 percent of the world's sugar. Did you know that in Minecraft, sugar cane is not just used to make food? You can craft it into paper and trade it with cartographer and librarian villagers.

TOP TIP

Granite makes up a lot of the real mountain as well as this Minecraft version.

Add small boats for tourists.

BEST BLOCKS

For a natural finish to your terraform, use blocks found in the world around you. In this jungle biome, that's granite, moss, and sand. You can also add extra earthy blocks, though, such as tuff, plus brown and green terracotta.

MOSS   **GRANITE**   **SAND**

SUGAR LOAF MOUNTAIN: CABLE CAR

Climbing up all 395 m (1,296 ft) of Sugar Loaf Mountain would take hours, but it takes just minutes by cable car – and the view is spectacular. The Sugar Loaf Cable Car makes the journey in two stages and runs every 30 minutes. Here's how you can recreate this iconic transport system in Minecraft.

BUILD TIP

This awesome build is a recreation of the cable cars and station on the mountain. The cable car can't actually move, but more complex models can be built using redstone and command blocks. This is an advanced way of building, so you'll need to research how to use them and then practise your skills on smaller builds first.

CABLE CAR STATIONS

First, you need to build your cable car stations. This build has three stations, each 17 blocks tall, 15 blocks wide, and 14 blocks deep. Once built, you can join the stations together with a custom cable made of andesite and iron bars.

The arch and steps are mostly made of andesite wall, deepslate, andesite stairs, and smooth stone slabs.

Add a powered rail, detector rail, and bell for realistic added details.

The platform is constructed mostly from stone bricks.

Crimson fence gates and planks add a burst of colour.

CABLES

The stations are joined together with a cable. Just like in Rio, this Minecraft version uses a two-tier cable system for extra safety: one cable is made of andesite stairs and slabs, and the other of iron bars. Use an anvil to hang the carriages to the cables.

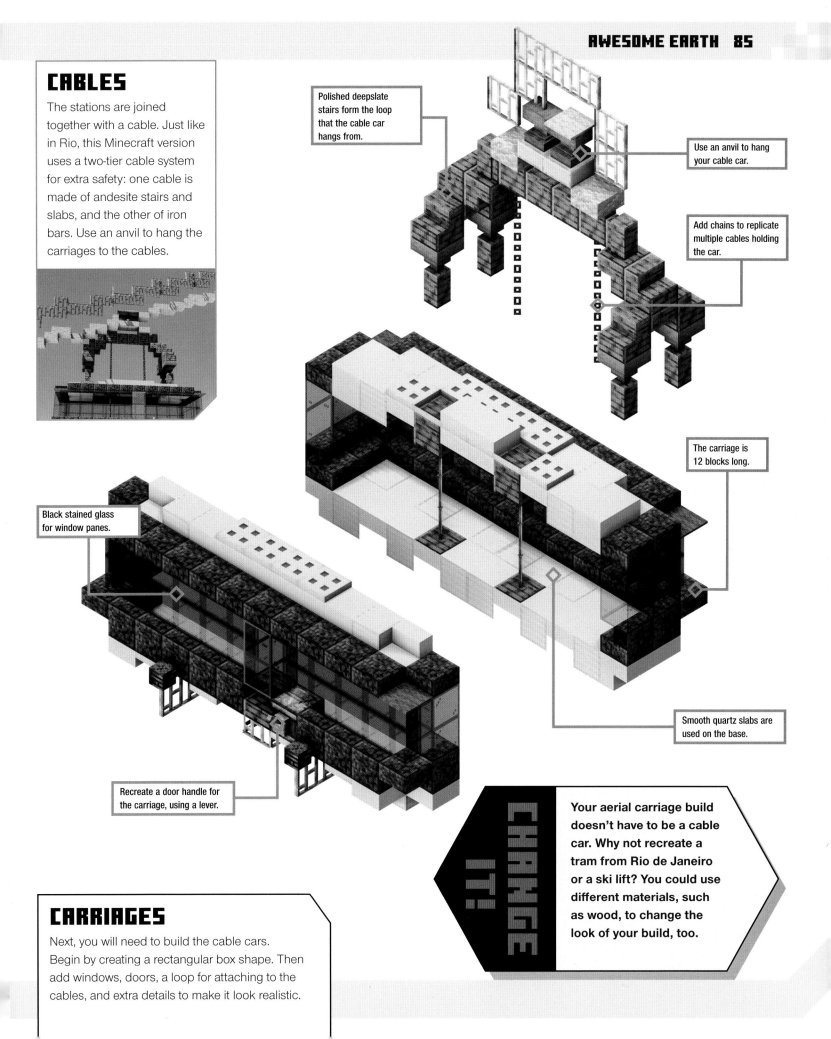

Polished deepslate stairs form the loop that the cable car hangs from.

Use an anvil to hang your cable car.

Add chains to replicate multiple cables holding the car.

The carriage is 12 blocks long.

Black stained glass for window panes.

Smooth quartz slabs are used on the base.

Recreate a door handle for the carriage, using a lever.

CHANGE IT!

Your aerial carriage build doesn't have to be a cable car. Why not recreate a tram from Rio de Janeiro or a ski lift? You could use different materials, such as wood, to change the look of your build, too.

CARRIAGES

Next, you will need to build the cable cars. Begin by creating a rectangular box shape. Then add windows, doors, a loop for attaching to the cables, and extra details to make it look realistic.

MOUNT ETNA

Volcanoes are the most powerful natural forces on Earth – and Mount Etna is one of the most active volcanoes in existence! Mount Etna is on the island of Sicily, off the coast of Italy. Its regular eruptions sometimes unleash rivers of liquid molten rock. Other times, they produce billowing ash clouds and lava bombs (lumps of lava which harden to form rocks). Legend says the volcano was the workshop of the Greek god Hephaestus, who used it to forge the weapons of the gods. Try building a forge next to your volcano in Minecraft, and use the lava to fuel a furnace.

LOOK CLOSER

Lava vents are small tunnels in a volcano that release streams of lava. They flow down the mountain and can be dangerous to the locals and wildlife below. To add lava vents to your Minecraft volcano, create a small hole and use a bucket of lava to place a lava source.

In Minecraft, lava is so hot that it can set fire to anything it touches.

The area around the volcano is barren. Use dead coral and dead bushes to show the lack of life.

Add mini trees made of dark oak fences and spruce leaves to recreate the forest beside the volcano.

In the real world, obsidian is a glassy rock formed when lava cools rapidly. In Minecraft, it is created when water flows over a lava source.

BEST BLOCKS

Volcanoes are naturally occuring geographical features, so in Minecraft they're best made from natural-looking blocks, such as cobbled deepslate, cobblestone, obsidian, and andesite. You'll need lots of magma, too!

COBBLED DEEPSLATE

MAGMA

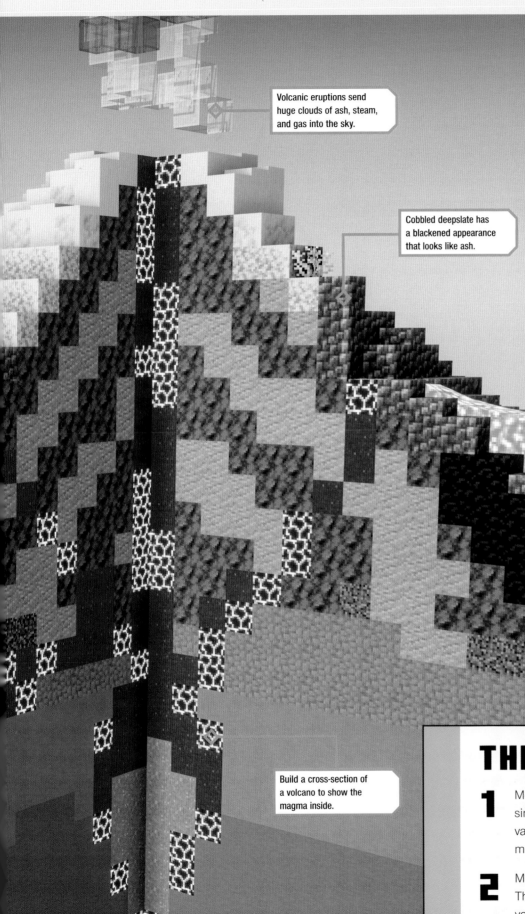

Volcanic eruptions send huge clouds of ash, steam, and gas into the sky.

Cobbled deepslate has a blackened appearance that looks like ash.

Build a cross-section of a volcano to show the magma inside.

SMOKE AND ASH

In the real world, erupting volcanoes send huge quantities of ash into the sky. The ash merges with clouds to form ash clouds, which can block sunlight and affect the weather. For your Minecraft volcano, use stained glass blocks to recreate a huge, billowing ash cloud. If you want a smaller ash cloud, you could place campfires beneath the surface blocks and then add lava on top of it to make it look like the volcano is producing smoke and ash.

THE REAL DEAL

1 Mount Etna has erupted almost 200 times since 1500. Its frequent eruptions act as a safety valve, releasing pressure that might cause even more dangerous and powerful eruptions.

2 Mount Etna emerged two million years ago. This makes it a young volcano – the oldest volcanoes have been dated to three billion years!

3 Although Mount Etna is an active volcano, it also has a popular hiking trail for tourists.

OKAVANGO DELTA

The vast Okavango Delta is located at the mouth of the Okavango River in Botswana, Africa. Every year, its grassy plains flood during the wet season, turning the area into a swampy wetland. Many different animals and plants thrive in the warm, wet conditions. Minecraft's swamp biome shares some similarities with the Okavango Delta, such as being home to a variety of wildlife and vegetation. Use a swamp biome as a basis to build your own version of the Okavango Delta and create a wetland paradise for Minecraft's mobs!

Build tall trees to replicate the baobab trees found in the delta.

LOOK CLOSER

There are a variety of frogs and toads living in the real Okavango Delta, from the giant African bullfrog to the long-nosed reed frog. In Minecraft, there are three frog variants, which vary according to the biome they come from. You can find orange frogs in a swamp biome. Just like real-world frogs, Minecraft frogs croak!

In the real world, flatboats are ideal for wetlands because they skim across the surface without being blocked by mud.

Add moss blocks to give the water a green tint.

Add adult frogs to your build or use a bucket to bring tadpoles from different swamps to grow into frogs.

Visitors can use their spyglasses to watch the local wildlife from a safe distance.

BEST BLOCKS

Swamp biomes provide a good source of clay and mud, as well as plant matter such as dead bushes. Add extra grass, clay, and mud to shape your swamp into a unique wetland. Use wood blocks to create your own dead trees.

GRASS

CLAY

MUD

Build a small passenger plane taking a scenic flight over the delta.

Dead trees are a common sight in the delta.

Use a combination of stairs and slabs on your safari lodge roof. Flip every second stairs block upside down to recreate this shape.

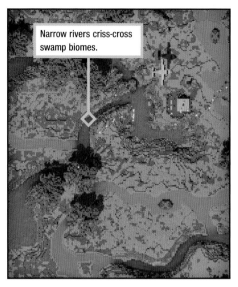

Narrow rivers criss-cross swamp biomes.

WETLAND LIFE

Minecraft's swamp biome has shallow water and lots of trees, such as oak and mangrove trees. The waters are full of seagrass and the ground is covered in tall grass. These water-logged conditions are similar to those in the Okavango Delta, where seasonal flooding of the grasslands provides an island oasis for nature.

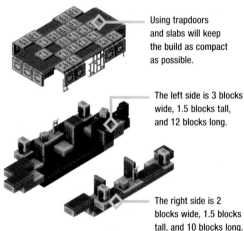

Using trapdoors and slabs will keep the build as compact as possible.

The left side is 3 blocks wide, 1.5 blocks tall, and 12 blocks long.

The right side is 2 blocks wide, 1.5 blocks tall, and 10 blocks long.

FLATBOAT

Travelling around in a wetland can be difficult due to the shallow water. Many boats get stuck in the mud. Build a flatboat to skim along the surface of the shallow waters in Minecraft. This flatboat sits a block below water level and is made of andesite variants, dark oak slabs, and spruce doors. Its roof is made of jungle trapdoors and brown carpets.

THE REAL DEAL

1 A delta is a wetland found at the mouth (end) of a river, where its water and sediment (pebbles, sand, and soil) flow into other rivers or the ocean.

2 The Okavango Delta is the world's largest inland delta and home to a range of wildlife, including hippos, elephants, lions, and birds.

3 During the wet season, the Okavango Delta can swell to be around 16,800 km² (6,500 sq miles).

OCEAN TRENCH

Oceans make up about 70 percent of the Earth's surface, but humans have explored only a fraction of them. The ocean floor is particularly mysterious, as the pressure there is too intense for humans to survive. What scientists do know is that the ocean floor is not flat – it has tall mountains and deep trenches. Not many creatures live there as few can survive in the cold, dark water. Venture down to the depths of Minecraft's oceans and build what you imagine might live there.

In Minecraft, you can swim to any depth underwater, as long as you have air.

Add colourful fish that thrive in hot water biomes.

Very little sunlight reaches these depths. In the real world, deep-sea creatures like squid lurk here. Recreate this by adding squid mobs to your build.

THE REAL DEAL

1 Oceans hold about 97 percent of the total water on Earth. There are five main oceans: the Pacific, Atlantic, Indian, Arctic, and Southern.

2 The Challenger Deep in the Mariana Trench is the deepest part of the ocean. It lies 11 km (7 miles) below the surface of the Pacific Ocean. That's deeper than the height of Mount Everest!

3 Peculiar creatures like the dumbo octopus, sea cucumbers, and fangtooth live in ocean trenches.

Use soul sand to make bubble columns, which provide air to breathe.

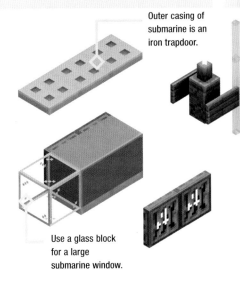

Outer casing of submarine is an iron trapdoor.

Use a glass block for a large submarine window.

SUBMARINE

Build a submarine in Minecraft to recreate the ones used to explore deep-sea trenches. This submarine is made from glass blocks, yellow terracotta, and trapdoors. The propeller is made of white stained glass panes, a red sandstone wall, and two acacia wall signs.

Use layers of stone, granite, andesite, cobbled deepslate, and mud to make the walls of the trench. You could add gold and emeralds for explorers to find, too.

Every underwater explorer needs a turtle shell helmet. In Survival mode, it will allow you to stay underwater for much longer than just holding your breath. Collect five scutes from turtles and then craft them into a helmet.

TOP TIP

TRENCH LIFE

Deep-sea trenches are full of amazing marine life. Bring your Minecraft trench to life with sea pickles, corals, seagrass, and kelp plants. Sea pickles, along with magma blocks, also provide enough light to be able to see. The deeper you go into the ocean, the stranger the creatures look. What kind of weird and wonderful creatures can you build?

BEST BLOCKS

Soul sand, along with magma, can be used to create bubble columns for underwater explorers. However, soul sand doesn't occur in the Overworld, so you'll need to travel to the Nether to collect some if you are playing in Survival mode.

MAGMA

SOUL SAND

REDWOOD FOREST

The tallest species of tree in the world is the giant redwood, reaching an average height of about 90 m (300 ft). If they were buildings, redwood trees would be more than 27 storeys high! Many giant redwoods are also extremely old – the oldest have been standing tall for more than 3,000 years. In Minecraft, the tallest trees grow in the jungle biome. Redwood trees don't spawn naturally, but you can just build your own. Head to a jungle biome to get started on creating a giant redwood forest.

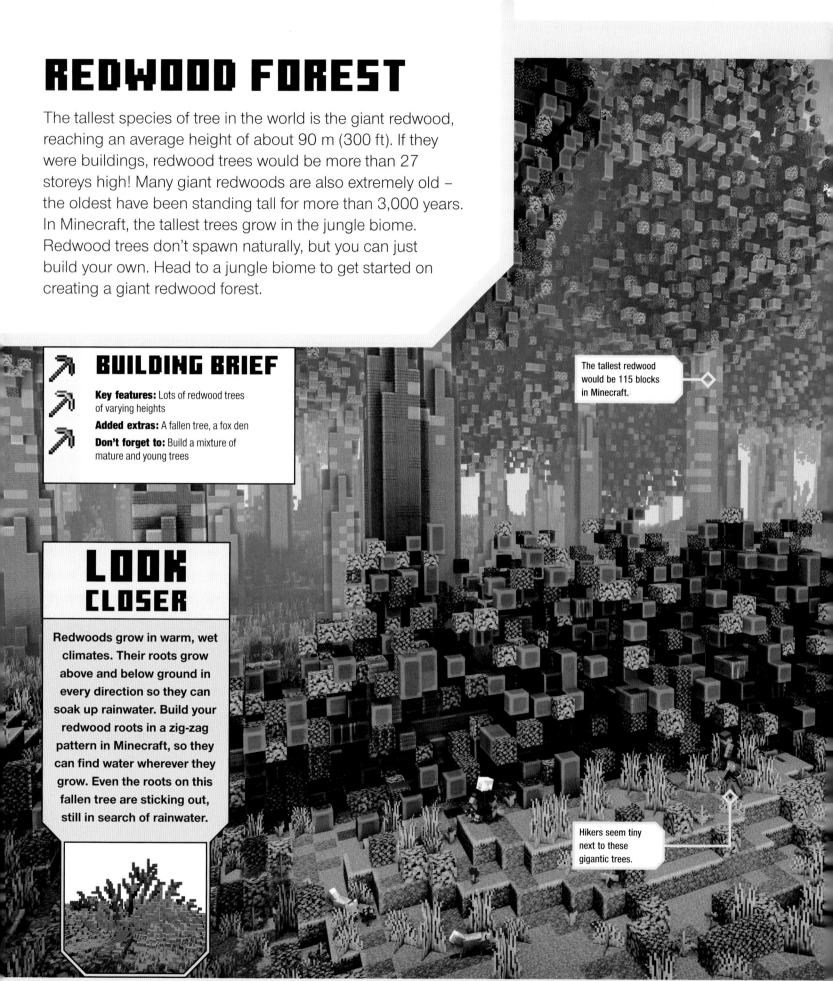

BUILDING BRIEF

Key features: Lots of redwood trees of varying heights

Added extras: A fallen tree, a fox den

Don't forget to: Build a mixture of mature and young trees

LOOK CLOSER

Redwoods grow in warm, wet climates. Their roots grow above and below ground in every direction so they can soak up rainwater. Build your redwood roots in a zig-zag pattern in Minecraft, so they can find water wherever they grow. Even the roots on this fallen tree are sticking out, still in search of rainwater.

The tallest redwood would be 115 blocks in Minecraft.

Hikers seem tiny next to these gigantic trees.

THE REAL DEAL

1 The tallest redwood can be found in Hyperion, USA. It stands at an astonishing 115.5 m (379 ft) tall with a diameter of over 20 m (65 ft).

2 Redwoods were used for construction in the 19th and 20th centuries, but the wood is soft and splinters easily.

3 California, USA, is famous for its vast redwood forests. The grand, ancient trees are a major tourist attraction.

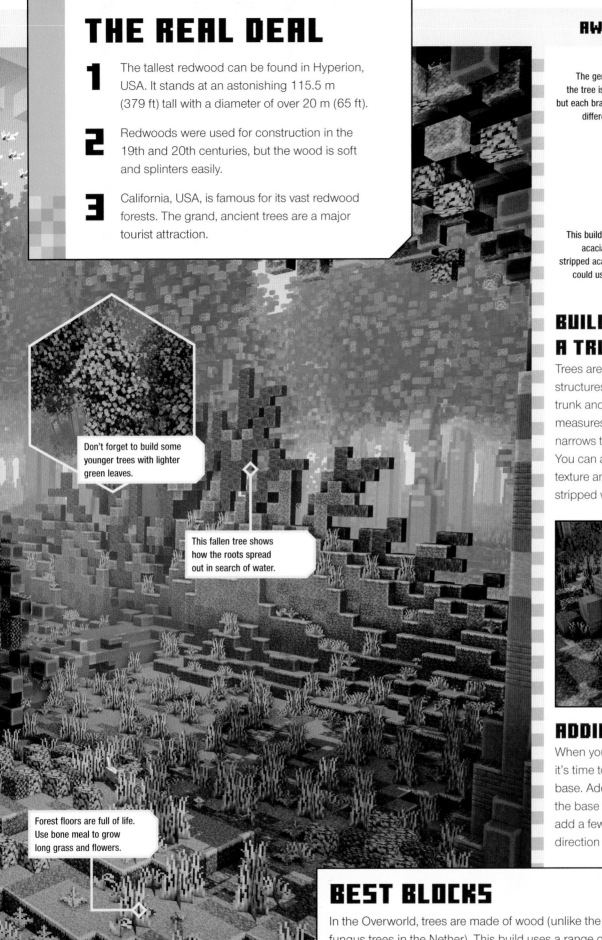

Don't forget to build some younger trees with lighter green leaves.

This fallen tree shows how the roots spread out in search of water.

Forest floors are full of life. Use bone meal to grow long grass and flowers.

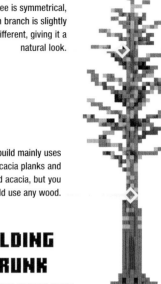

The general shape of the tree is symmetrical, but each branch is slightly different, giving it a natural look.

This build mainly uses acacia planks and stripped acacia, but you could use any wood.

BUILDING A TRUNK

Trees are super easy structures to build. Simply start with the trunk and then build upwards. This trunk measures 5x5 blocks at the base and narrows to just one block wide at the top. You can add planks to create a bark-like texture and also use an axe to create stripped wood.

ADDING ROOTS

When your tree trunk is big and tall, it's time to add some details to the base. Add a few plank blocks around the base of the tree to widen it, then add a few more blocks leading in each direction to create roots.

BEST BLOCKS

In the Overworld, trees are made of wood (unlike the fungus trees in the Nether). This build uses a range of acacia and jungle wood block variants to create both young and old redwood trees. The canopy is made of green terracotta and azalea leaves.

ACACIA PLANKS

JUNGLE PLANKS

GALÁPAGOS ISLANDS

The Galápagos Islands are famous for their amazing wildlife. Located off the coast of Ecuador in the Pacific Ocean, this archipelago, or chain of islands, contains 13 large islands and six smaller ones. The islands feature volcanoes, jungles, and beaches, as well as unusual animal life like marine iguanas and giant tortoises. You won't find these animals in Minecraft, so get creative with turtles and parrots while crafting and building your own island paradise.

BEST BLOCKS

You're going to need lots of blocks to build the islands. Sand, grass, and stone all work well, but the Galápagos is volcanic, so this build also uses lots of tuff and deepslate for its volcanic craters.

TUFF

DEEPSLATE

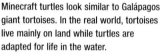

Minecraft turtles look similar to Galápagos giant tortoises. In the real world, tortoises live mainly on land while turtles are adapted for life in the water.

There are 21 volcanoes above sea level on the Galápagos Islands. Will you include that many in your build?

Add a small boat made of crimson slabs and stairs to deliver supplies to the port village.

BUILD TIP

You can find a group of islands in Minecraft by searching, or you can create your own. When lava is mixed with water, it creates cobblestone. Use this trick to imitate the real way islands are made and start your archipelago.

In Minecraft, coral reefs can be placed in cold or warm water biomes.

Create a micro house by placing a block and adding a trapdoor as a rooftop.

PORT VILLAGE

The largest Galápagos island is called Isabella. It is home to a small port village, a bit like this one in Minecraft. The village is very small, with only a few buildings, including some houses and a gift shop. Despite its size, Isabella is an important centre for fishing and tourism, so be sure to include boats and a dock in your Minecraft build as well.

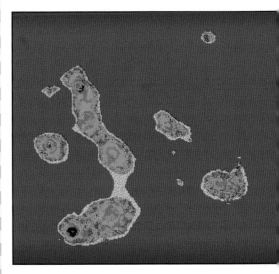

VOLCANIC ISLANDS

The Galápagos archipelago was formed by volcanic activity, so you can have lots of fun incorporating volcanoes and volcanic features such as lava and craters in your build. Make each island a little different in size, shape, and character. For instance, the most active volcano, which has regular eruptions, is on the island of Ferdinanda. You could recreate this volcanic island with lots of glowing red lava.

THE REAL DEAL

1 The Galápagos is home to some species, such as the giant tortoise that are not found anywhere else. In Spanish, *galápago* means tortoise.

2 The archipelago is 1,000 km (600 miles) from the nearest landmass (Ecuador). This helps to protect its unique ecosystem.

3 Scientist Charles Darwin developed his famous theory of evolution after studying the plants and animals of the Galápagos Islands.

HA LONG BAY

The limestone pillars of Ha Long Bay in Vietnam stand out like jewels in the glistening waters. This tropical paradise is full of rainforests, caves, and coral reefs, and is home to many species of fish and animals. There are only a few small floating villages in this UNESCO World Heritage site. Build your own fantastic fishing village in Minecraft – and don't forget to craft a boat to travel back to the mainland, too.

BUILDING BRIEF

Key features: Floating villages, tall limestone structures, fishing boats

Added extras: Deep caves

Don't forget to: Add lighting with sea pickles

LOOK CLOSER

Ha Long Bay has huge underground caves to explore. Inside these caves are rock formations called stalagmites and stalactites, which are formed by dripping water. In Minecraft, stalagmites and stalactites are made from pointed dripstone, and can be found in dripstone caves.

Add moss or vines to cobblestone to recreate the karsts' aged look.

Use trapdoors for windows. Light will flood in through the gaps.

Build simple homes on oxidized copper blocks. The blue block colour blends in with the water so the houses appear to be floating.

THE REAL DEAL

1 Legend has it that dragons once lived in this bay. In fact, the name Ha Long translates as "descending dragon".

2 Ha Long Bay is home to some of the rarest animals in the world, such as the white-headed langur, which is found only on Cat Ba Island.

3 Fishing villages have been a way of life for the locals for a long time. They have been here for thousands of years.

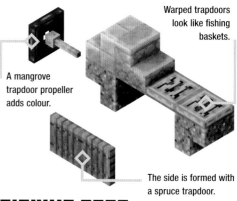

A mangrove trapdoor propeller adds colour.

Warped trapdoors look like fishing baskets.

The side is formed with a spruce trapdoor.

FISHING BOAT

A fishing village needs fishing boats! This six-block-long design is simple to build and looks great in the water. The trapdoor propeller even sticks out of the water. Create a whole fleet of fishing boats.

Use a mix of mossy cobblestone, calcite, andesite, and diorite to create natural-looking karsts.

Slabs and trapdoors can be used to create walkways that sit just above water level.

Spot dolphins in the tropical waters!

TOWER KARST

Karst is the name given to a landscape made of limestone. There's no limestone in Minecraft, so you'll need to be creative to build a tower karst like those seen in Ha Long Bay. Start by building a big rock from andesite and add some streaks of diorite and calcite for a unique appearance. Finally, finish it off with greenery, such as mossy cobblestone and leaves.

BEST BLOCKS

In Survival mode, finding enough wood in an ocean biome is a challenge. You can grow your own trees using bone meal and saplings to save time. These floating villages use wood block variants such as jungle, acacia, and mangrove planks.

JUNGLE PLANKS

MANGROVE PLANKS

ACACIA PLANKS

MARBLE CAVES

Along the border of Argentina and Chile there is a natural geological wonder unlike any other – a set of stunning and intricate marble caves that glow a glistening blue. The Marble Caves were formed by the waves of General Carrera Lake, which slowly wore away and sculpted the marble. Their brilliant blue colour is actually the water reflecting on the rock. Thrill your friends by creating a unique cave for them to find in Minecraft. While there are no marble blocks in Minecraft, you can use a variety of other blocks to achieve the beautiful blue glow.

BUILDING BRIEF

Key features: Large blue caverns

Added extras: Canoes in a range of different colours

Don't forget to: Add End rods to your cave to give the water a shimmering glow

Make unique stalactites from an End rod and iron bar.

Place glow lichen on the sides of other blocks to emit light.

End rods cast a pearlescent light.

LOOK CLOSER

The magic of this cave is that wherever you look there's something going on. Almost every block adds a different blue or white shade, from glazed terracotta variants, to diorite walls, and even candles. The candles also light up every corner to stop mobs from spawning.

BEST BLOCKS

To build glistening blue caves of your own, use blue and blue-green blocks such as blue, light blue, and cyan concrete, warped wart, and prismarine.

BLUE CONCRETE

CYAN CONCRETE

WARPED WART

PRISMARINE

THE REAL DEAL

1 The pristine General Carrera Lake is one of the largest lakes by area in South America, at 1,850 km² (710 sq miles).

2 The Marble Caves took a very long time to form. Experts estimate as many as 6,000 years.

3 The blue colour of the caves is at its brightest in the summer when the ice melts and the lake's water level rises.

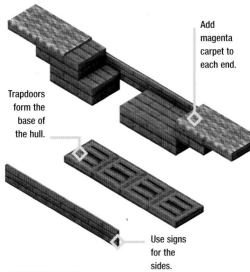

Add magenta carpet to each end.

Trapdoors form the base of the hull.

Use signs for the sides.

CANOES

To preserve this natural wonder, tourists visit the caves in canoes and boats. Create some colourful canoes to add to your build. This one is made using crimson pieces, but you can make yours any colour you like.

STALACTITES

Water dripping from the ceiling of the Marble Caves for thousands of years has created lots of unique natural features, such as stalactites. In Minecraft, stalactites can be crafted from pointed dripstone, but you can get extra creative with these custom-made ones. These stalactites use a variety of blocks including glass panes, diorite walls, iron bars, and even cobwebs.

Players can admire the beautiful caves from a canoe.

Create light-blue water by building your cave in a warm ocean biome and filling the sea floor with blue blocks.

PLITVICE LAKES

Located by the Dinaric Alps mountains in Croatia, the landscape of the Plitvice Lakes National Park has formed gradually over thousands of years. Water from rain and rivers has shaped the limestone and chalk rocks into amazing lakes, caves, and waterfalls. There are 16 lakes in the national park, connected by walkways to allow visitors to explore, so this would be a major natural project to embark on in Minecraft. Search for a jungle biome with lakes and waterfalls, and use a lake you find there to get started on your own national park.

BUILDING BRIEF

Key features: Colourful lakes and waterfalls connected by wooden walkways

Added extras: Mobs such as wolves, axolotls, and frogs

Don't forget to: Add white water to your waterfalls

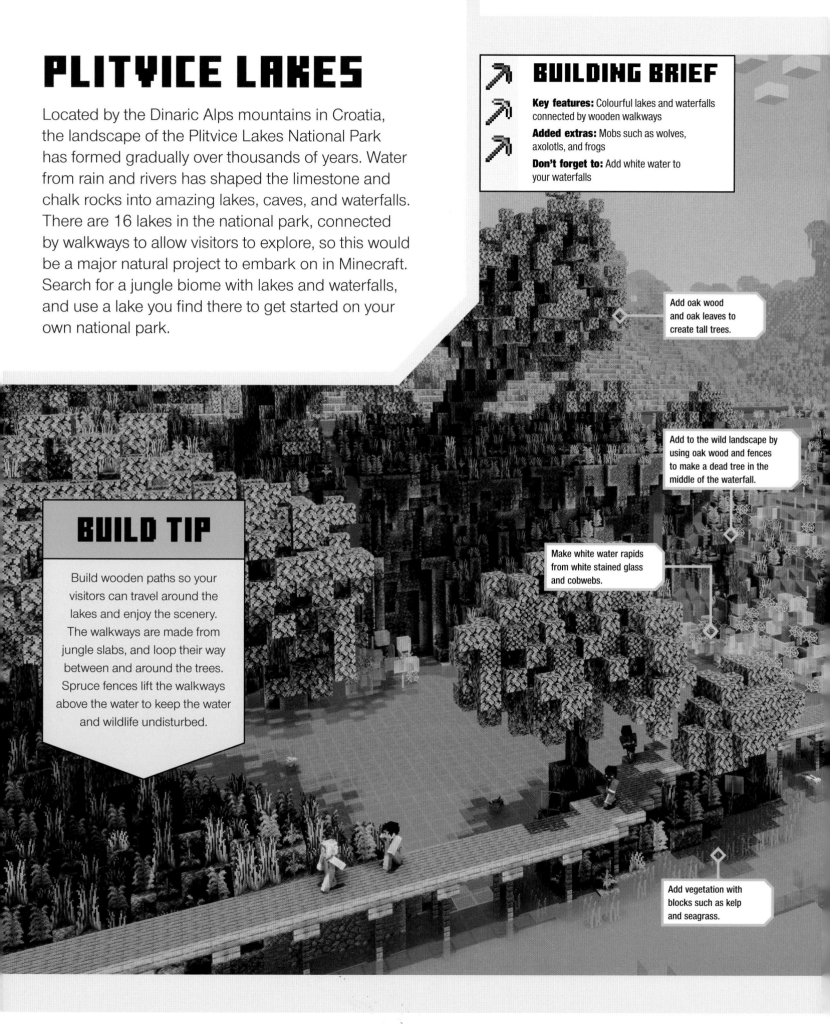

Add oak wood and oak leaves to create tall trees.

Add to the wild landscape by using oak wood and fences to make a dead tree in the middle of the waterfall.

Make white water rapids from white stained glass and cobwebs.

Add vegetation with blocks such as kelp and seagrass.

BUILD TIP

Build wooden paths so your visitors can travel around the lakes and enjoy the scenery. The walkways are made from jungle slabs, and loop their way between and around the trees. Spruce fences lift the walkways above the water to keep the water and wildlife undisturbed.

THE REAL DEAL

1 Plitvice Lakes change colour from blue to green depending on the levels of minerals and algae in them and the angle of the sun.

2 The national park is home to a diverse range of mammals, including bears, lynxes, otters, wild boars, deer, wolves, foxes, badgers, and bats.

3 The park is also home to more than 160 species of birds, such as owls, hawks, woodpeckers, and cuckoos.

WHITE WATER

When water flows quickly over rocks and cliffs it becomes rough and splashy, and appears white and frothy. This turbulent water effect is recreated in this build with cyan and blue stained glass blocks and panes. The addition of cobwebs creates an even splashier effect!

Surround your waterfalls with lush forests and grasslands. In the real national park the lakes make up only 1 percent of the area!

In winter, the waterfalls at the real Plitvice lakes can freeze over. Why not make a frozen version of your Minecraft national park?

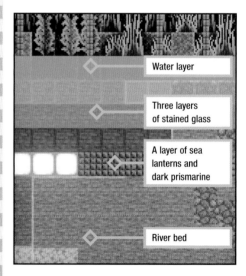

Water layer

Three layers of stained glass

A layer of sea lanterns and dark prismarine

River bed

Add animals, such as axolotls and frogs, to the build.

COLOURFUL LAKES

Each biome has a different water colour. This lake is in a jungle biome, where lakes are light blue. However, you can change the colour of your lake depending on the way you build your lake bed. For a turquoise lake, you'll need three types of blocks in layers: one layer of dark prismarine and sea lanterns, three of stained glass blocks in white, light blue, and blue, and one of water. When viewed from above, these blocks give the waters a unique colour.

BEST BLOCKS

To create your lake bed in Survival mode, you'll need a beach or desert for sand to craft glass blocks and an ocean monument for dark prismarine. The rest of the build uses all the blocks you would find in a jungle biome.

DARK PRISMARINE

GO EXPLORE

Take off on an adventure – and travel the world one page at a time! Visit a bustling bazaar, a beautiful floating village, and a panda sanctuary. Explore new ways to get around, from boats and trains to a powerful rocket, and discover how you can use Minecraft's diverse blocks to build the real world. Ready, set, explore!

THE DANCING HOUSE

If you're looking for inspiration for an extraordinary build, check out the Dancing House in Prague, Czechia (Czech Republic). It is designed to look like two people dancing. The "dancer" on the right has 99 concrete panels of different shapes and sizes, while the "dancer" on the left is made from glass and steel pillars. For your next Minecraft model, throw out the rule book and build something unique of your own, with crazy curves, unusual materials, or amazing angles. What kind of building will you create?

BUILDING BRIEF

Key features: Mix of shapes and materials (including stone and glass), lots of windows

Added extras: Roof garden, amazing interiors

Don't forget to: Think about the relationship between the different parts of the building

THE REAL DEAL

1 The Dancing House is built in a style known as "deconstructivism". This style breaks traditional building rules about angles and symmetry.

2 A large, twisted iron structure sits on top. It is known as "Medusa" – named after the Gorgon from Greek mythology who had snakes for hair.

3 The Dancing House has an art gallery, a restaurant, and a rooftop bar. It also includes a hotel with 40 rooms for people to stay in.

> Iron bars are ideal for creating statues and sculptures. Placing an iron bar against a block creates a half-block-wide wall; placing two beside each other creates a wall; and placing just one creates a standing rod.

TOP TIP

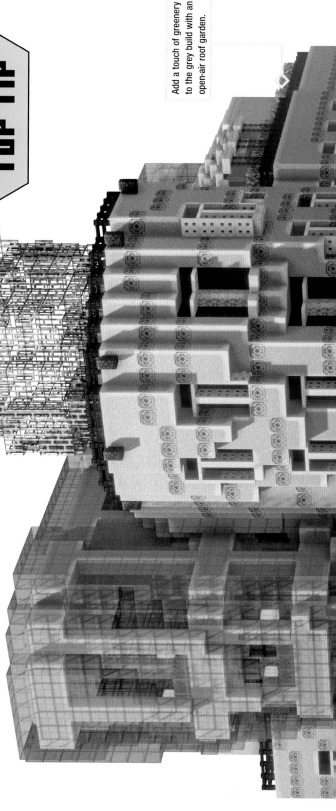

Add a touch of greenery to the grey build with an open-air roof garden.

BUILD HIGHLIGHTS

Wonky windows make it hard to see how many floors there are.

The glass tower representing the dancer on the left is "squeezed" to half its width at the centre. It looks like the dancer is bending!

Using lots of glass blocks will fill your building with light.

The first floor is extra high above ground. Recreate this so that horse-riding players can easily pass underneath.

AMAZING INTERIORS

Let your imagination run free for the interiors, too. This build makes clever use of some unusual materials. The bed frame is made from signs, while the mattress is wool blocks. Corals may not be so colourful out of the water, but they can make a luxurious, fluffy carpet. A dragon egg with a froglight shade makes a stylish bedside lamp.

BEST BLOCKS

This build uses lots of clay blocks for its light greyish-blue colour. Lodestones, with their ringed texture, have been placed along the walls to recreate the exposed framework.

LODESTONE

CLAY

SHINJUKU

The busy and colourful Shinjuku area of Toyko, Japan, is like a city within a city. The neon-lit metropolis is bustling with life and is known for its fancy hotels and restaurants. You'll also find market stalls selling popular foods such as sushi, soba, and ramen. There are endless entertainment options, including shopping, karaoke, and dancing clubs. What fun activities will you build into your ideal city?

Building in Survival mode? Use concrete powder. This block is easier to mine than concrete, allowing you to experiment with your build. When you're happy with your work, use a water bucket to transform it into concrete.

TOP TIP

BUILDING BRIEF

Key features: Tall tower blocks, large roads, colourful lights

Added extras: Glazed terracotta designs

Don't forget to: Light up the inside of buildings to prevent mobs from spawning in dark corners

Add captivating colours to the city with diamond and prismarine blocks.

Use sea lanterns, End rods, froglights, and shroomlights to cast Shinjuku in an electrifying neon glow.

THE REAL DEAL

1 Shinjuku Station is the busiest train station in the world! It has a whopping 200 exits.

2 You can take the metro from Shinjuku to one of Tokyo's other stations to catch a bullet train (*Shinkansen*). These high-speed electric trains carry nearly one million passengers each day.

3 Shinjuku has the largest bus terminal in Japan. You can catch a long-haul bus from the area to 39 of Japan's 47 prefectures (districts).

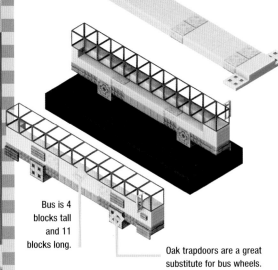

Bus is 4 blocks tall and 11 blocks long.

Oak trapdoors are a great substitute for bus wheels.

PUBLIC BUS

Traffic is a major issue in big cities like Tokyo. Too many vehicles fill the air with pollution. Make your Minecraft city more environmentally and pedestrian friendly with buses. This bus is made of smooth quartz, but you could use bamboo to make yours look like a yellow school bus.

Tall buildings maximize the use of city space. Place redstone lights at the top of your towers, so that they can be seen by elytra-riders!

Make street signs from magenta glazed terracotta with an arrow added to each side.

Use mangrove trapdoors for your car wheels.

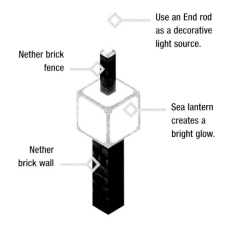

Use an End rod as a decorative light source.

Nether brick fence

Sea lantern creates a bright glow.

Nether brick wall

STREETLIGHTS

Remember to place lights in your builds. This streetlight has a two-block-tall Nether brick wall so that players can pass below them.

BEST BLOCKS

To build a busy metropolis you need to start with the foundations: roads, pavements, and buildings. Concrete, light blue terracotta, and stone block variants work well for these.

CONCRETE **LIGHT BLUE TERRACOTTA** **STONE**

FLOATING VILLAGE

Tonlé Sap in Cambodia is the largest freshwater lake in Southeast Asia – and it is home to more than 170 colourful floating villages. Thousands of people live in these floating homes, which are built to cope with the rising and falling water levels of the vast lake. In Minecraft, floating villages can be built anywhere there is water. Consider which waters you want to live in. Minecraft's waters are mostly different shades of blue, but you'll find them in grey-green if you choose a swamp biome, like this one.

BUILDING BRIEF

Key features: Colourful floating houses on stilts

Added extras: Boats, animal mobs

Don't forget to: Use a variety of colours for the different houses

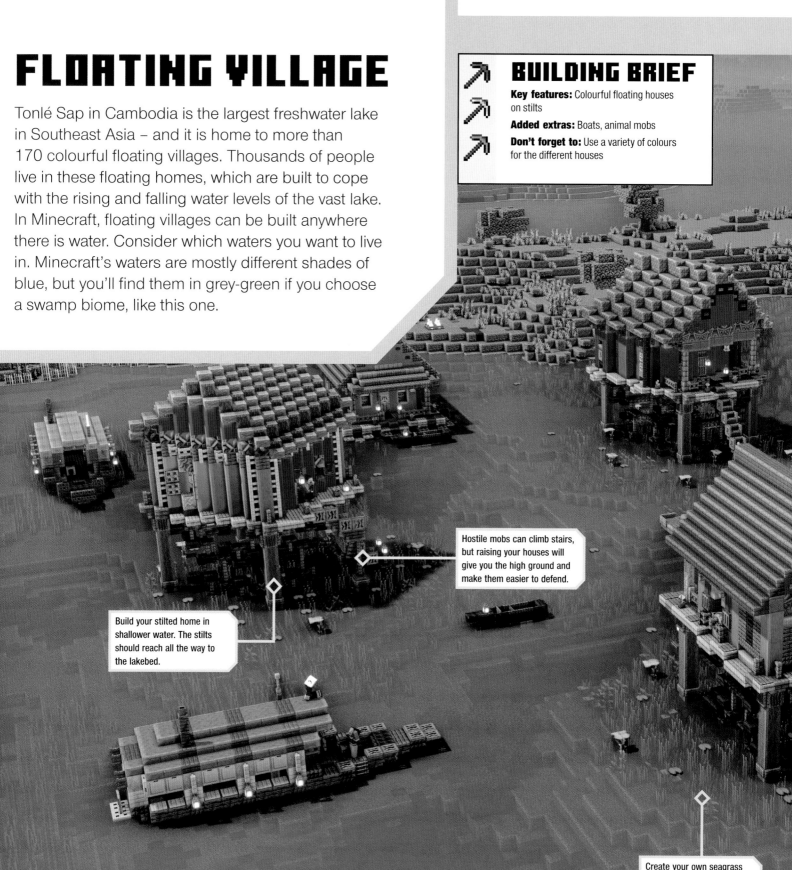

Hostile mobs can climb stairs, but raising your houses will give you the high ground and make them easier to defend.

Build your stilted home in shallower water. The stilts should reach all the way to the lakebed.

Create your own seagrass using bone meal on the underwater blocks.

BEST BLOCKS

These homes use lots of dyed terracotta and glazed terracotta to stand out against the dark water. In Survival mode, you can craft glazed terracotta by smelting dyed terracotta blocks.

BROWN GLAZED TERRACOTTA

LIME GLAZED TERRACOTTA

THE REAL DEAL

1 In the wet season, the lake is around 14,000 km² (5,405 sq miles) and over 8 m (26 ft) deep. In the dry season, it's 2,800 square km (1,081 sq miles) and just 1 m (3 ft) or 2 m (6 ft) deep.

2 The lake drains into the Mekong River in the dry season. In the wet season, an unusual phenomenon occurs where it flows in the opposite direction to form an enormous lake.

3 Fishing is an important industry for those living in the floating villages around Tonlé Sap.

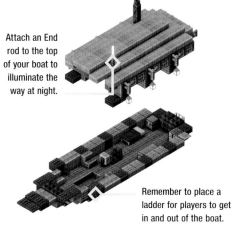

Attach an End rod to the top of your boat to illuminate the way at night.

Remember to place a ladder for players to get in and out of the boat.

Use bright colours to help you find your way around.

GETTING AROUND

You'll need a boat to navigate a floating village. The base of this boat is made from spruce planks and various stairs, plus ladders, trapdoors, and fences. Add a protective roof using blocks such as cut red sandstone and prismarine. Use coloured blocks throughout, like oxidized copper and crimson stairs, to make your boat as colourful as your houses.

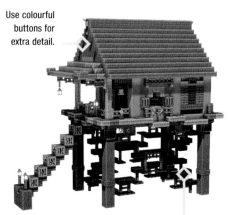

Use colourful buttons for extra detail.

Add docking platforms at different heights so boats can visit no matter the level of tide.

LIVING ON WATER

Stilted houses are ideal for living on the lake as they are less likely to flood when the water level rises. This Minecraft house stands atop a set of four 8-block-tall stripped spruce logs stilts, which keep it above water level. It has high and low level boat docking platforms made from spruce fences, dark oak trapdoors, and slabs. The spruce stairs and warped trapdoor staircase is also long enough for low tides.

> **You can travel between any of the floating villages by boat. If you're playing in Survival mode, just make sure you're home before nightfall when hostile mobs start to spawn. Be especially wary of drowned!**
>
> ## TOP TIP

LONDON TUBE STATION

Traffic in big cities can make travelling around very slow, so many of them have underground railway networks to help people get around. The first underground railway in the world was built in 1863 in London. Nicknamed "the Tube," it now covers 402 km (250 miles) and has more than 1 billion passengers every year. This Minecraft Tube station is complex, but worth the effort as you can also use many elements of this build in your other projects. A bubble lift works well in any tall building.

BUILDING BRIEF

Key features: Underground station and train

Added extras: Escalator, signs, bubble lift (see more on p113)

Don't forget to: Research real-life stations for colours and details

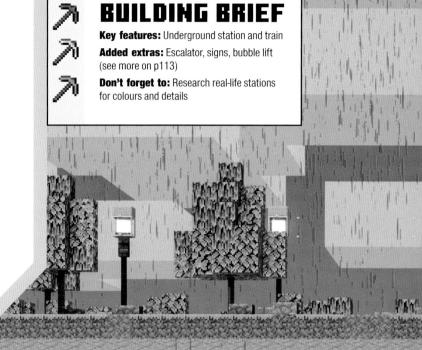

In Survival mode, digging tunnels for an underground railway is a time-consuming project. Create an enchanting table and enchant a pickaxe with Efficiency to save you time.

TOP TIP

Red, white, and blue are the iconic colours of the London Underground.

THE REAL DEAL

1 The London Underground has 270 stations and 11 different lines serving London and its suburbs.

2 Early Tube trains were steam trains. Routes were built in shallow tunnels and needed plenty of vents for the steam and smoke to escape. They were replaced by electric locomotives from 1890.

3 Waterloo is the Tube network's busiest station, with 100.3 million passengers per year.

BUILD HIGHLIGHTS

Stations are full of big open spaces. You can add lots of small builds to fill the area and make it more interesting. Escalators and vending machines are perfect, but why stop there? Experiment with columns, notice boards, and so much more.

Use dark prismarine stairs along with warped fence gates, and warped signs to provide seats for waiting commuters.

Bring the station to life with real-world features such as this vending machine.

Build a bubble lift like this one to bring passengers to and from the platform.

These anvil and deepslate tile stair train tracks look super realistic.

ESCALATOR

Escalators take passengers to and from the train platforms. These Minecraft ones are static and made with polished andesite stairs, andesite walls, and cyan stained glass panes. You could experiment with redstone if you want to get really creative.

VENDING MACHINE

Journeys go much quicker when you're munching on a snack! Create your own vending machine with bookshelves and a tripwire hook. Use a button for the dispenser.

BEST BLOCKS

Pick a real-world station and choose blocks that match its colours and textures. The trains at this station have a white, blue, and red concrete design.

BLUE CONCRETE

RED CONCRETE

LONDON TUBE STATION: GETTING IN AND OUT

Inner-city commuters always seem to be in a rush. They need the most time-efficient journey to help them reach their destinations, so your Minecraft station needs to operate as smoothly and efficiently as possible. Check out these two cool features, which will help passengers enter and exit the station as quickly as possible.

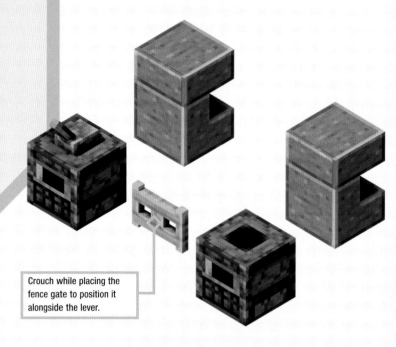

Crouch while placing the fence gate to position it alongside the lever.

TICKETS, PLEASE!

Skip the queues and build a working ticket gate for your station. With this ticket gate, players simply walk up, pull the lever, and walk onto the train platform.

GATES

The ticket gate uses only a smoker, fence gate, and lever. Repeat this design to create a row of gates leading onto the platform.

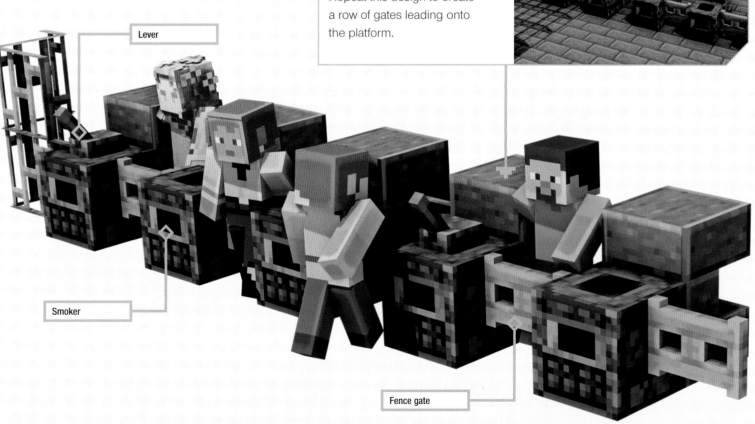

Lever

Smoker

Fence gate

BUBBLE LIFT

To create a bubble lift, you need water, kelp, dirt, magma, and soul sand, plus some building blocks. Start by building two vertical 3x3 block columns and filling them with water. Place a dirt block at the base of each column and fill the columns with kelp (use bone meal to rapidly grow the kelp). Replace the dirt blocks with soul sand at the bottom of one column and magma at the bottom of the other (this will break the kelp). You now have an upward and downward bubble column!

WHICH FLOOR?

Create entrances to the bubble lift on each floor using open fence gates. Fence gates will also prevent the water from flooding out.

BUILD TIP

You could build a regular staircase to get to and from the train platform, but bubble lifts are one of the fastest ways to climb vertically in Minecraft. You can use them for underground mines and bases, and they are an essential component of many automatic mob farms.

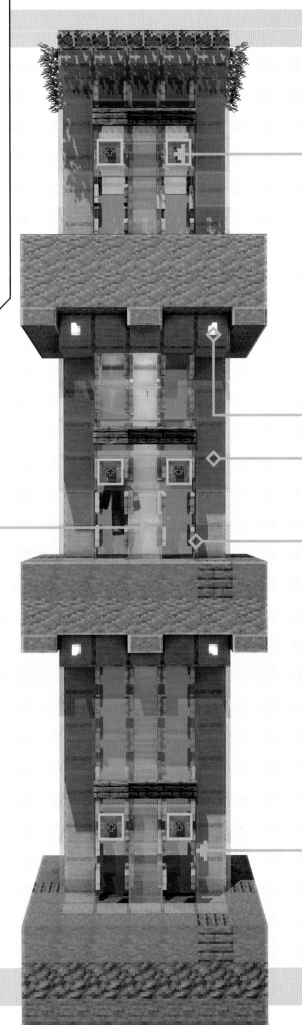

UP AND DOWN

Add magenta glazed terracotta arrows to show whether the lift is going up or down. You can also decorate the structure, if you want to.

Add lighting using End rods.

This is 25 blocks tall and 5 blocks deep.

Step into the water to enter the bubble lift.

GLASS LIFT

Glass blocks look impressive and also allow players to see whether the lift is in use. This model uses cyan and light blue stained glass and smooth stone for a sleek, modern look. Which colour glass will you use for yours?

UROS ISLANDS

Lake Titicaca is the second largest lake in South America. It is also one of Earth's most ancient lakes, and is thought to be more than 3 million years old. Over the last 3,700 years, the Uros people have made their homes on the lake by building floating islands made of hand-woven totora reeds. Have you ever settled in an ocean biome? You can build your own floating islands using hay bales and then add houses and other buildings, such as shops, or a school to create a village.

BUILDING BRIEF

Key features: A floating island and houses made of renewable hay bales

Added extras: Plants, mobs, and boats

Don't forget to: Plant a crop of wheat seeds for hay bales

Have fun creating different shaped buildings to represent houses, a school, shops, a church, and more.

Add lookout towers to your islands.

Recreating one of the Uros islands in Minecraft uses lots of reed-like hay bales. Hay bales look different, depending which side you can see. Use the red-lined side for houses and the yellow side for the island itself.

TOP TIP

The Uros people's boats are made from reeds. This Minecraft version is made from hay bales, crimson trapdoors, and oak variants.

THE REAL DEAL

1 Reeds are essential to the Uros people. Preparing the reeds goes through three stages: collecting, drying, and weaving.

2 The Uros people use reeds to create many things, including boats. They are expert weavers, and make textiles to sell.

3 The islands are constructed from layers of reeds, which need to be replaced before they rot. The ground feels soft and springy.

A wheat farm provides all the wheat needed for the community.

Use hay bales to look like drying wheat.

Reeds grow around the islands. You can use leaf blocks, azalea, and bamboo to recreate these.

CROPS

Collecting enough building materials can be an arduous task, but the Uros people have found the perfect solution. They grow their own! Recreate an Uros farm with a seed farm that provides an endless source of wheat for hay bales. It is also self-renewing, as harvested wheat provides more seeds to plant.

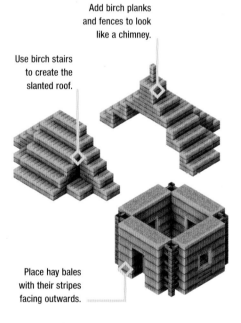

Add birch planks and fences to look like a chimney.

Use birch stairs to create the slanted roof.

Place hay bales with their stripes facing outwards.

BEST BLOCKS

Hay bales are ideal for recreating the reeds used by the Uros people. Use lots of hay bales and wheat farms to capture this reed-focused way of life.

HAY BALE

THATCH HOUSES

The Uros people live in houses made of reeds. In this build they have been recreated using hay bales with the striped sides showing outwards. The roof uses similar yellow-looking birch block variants.

CHENGDU PANDA BASE

Our planet is full of wildlife. Unfortunately, some of this wildlife is endangered. Around the world, centres have opened in an effort to preserve and support endangered animals. China's Chengdu Research Base of Giant Panda Breeding has made great strides in renewing populations of giant pandas. There are representations of many endangered animals in Minecraft. How will you help preserve them?

BUILDING BRIEF

Key features: Platforms, fences, vines, and ladders

Added extras: Platforms at different heights

Don't forget to: Include enough bamboo for the pandas to eat

Stone stairs recreate Chinese garden decor.

There's a small chance that a baby panda in Minecraft will drop a slimeball when it sneezes!

Add ladders to your structure. Minecraft pandas climb ladders when they push up against them.

BEST BLOCKS

Building a wildlife research centre is all about catering for the animals that live there. This panda base is built using mostly jungle slabs, trapdoors, stripped logs, and lots of bamboo of course!

STRIPPED JUNGLE LOG

JUNGLE SLAB

THE REAL DEAL

1 The giant panda is China's national animal. China dedicates a lot of resources to ensure that its numbers increase.

2 Chengdu is the ancestral home of pandas. Preserved remains show that they have lived in this part of the world for more than 4,000 years.

3 Chengdu Research Base was founded with six rescue pandas in the 1980s. With breeding efforts, that number had grown to 237 by 2023.

Pandas have poor eyesight. Light your Minecraft base with dim soul lanterns so they don't strain their eyes.

Feeding two pandas bamboo in Minecraft will encourage them to breed.

To breed pandas, there must be at least one bamboo that is 8 blocks tall within 5 blocks of two pandas.

Use jungle trapdoors to add interesting textures to your platforms.

In Minecraft, pandas have secret "genes". They can be normal, lazy, worried, playful, weak, or aggressive.

DO YOUR RESEARCH

Research your chosen animal or animals to provide the best environment for them. Pandas are very rare in Minecraft — they can only be found in jungle biomes. They love bamboo, which grows on grass, dirt, mycelium, podzol, sand, and mud. Although podzol is common in jungle biomes, pandas cannot spawn on it, so avoid using too much if you want to encourage breeding.

FUN AND GAMES

It's important to make sure the animals are happy. Chengdu Research Base provides games and elements of the wild for the pandas, such as platforms, ladders and vines to climb, and bamboo. How will you entertain your pandas to keep them active and happy?

ROVOS RAIL

Sometimes you don't want to get where you're going fast – you want to journey in style. Rail travel doesn't get any more stylish than an old-fashioned steam train. On Rovos Rail, passengers can travel through some of southern Africa's most stunning landscapes in luxurious carriages pulled by a locomotive. Recreate an elegant Rovos Rail train in Minecraft, or maybe research and build a classic steam train from the past instead.

BUILDING BRIEF

Key features: Steam locomotive, carriages (see more on p120–121)

Added extras: Passengers and wildlife

Don't forget to: Build in a scenic biome

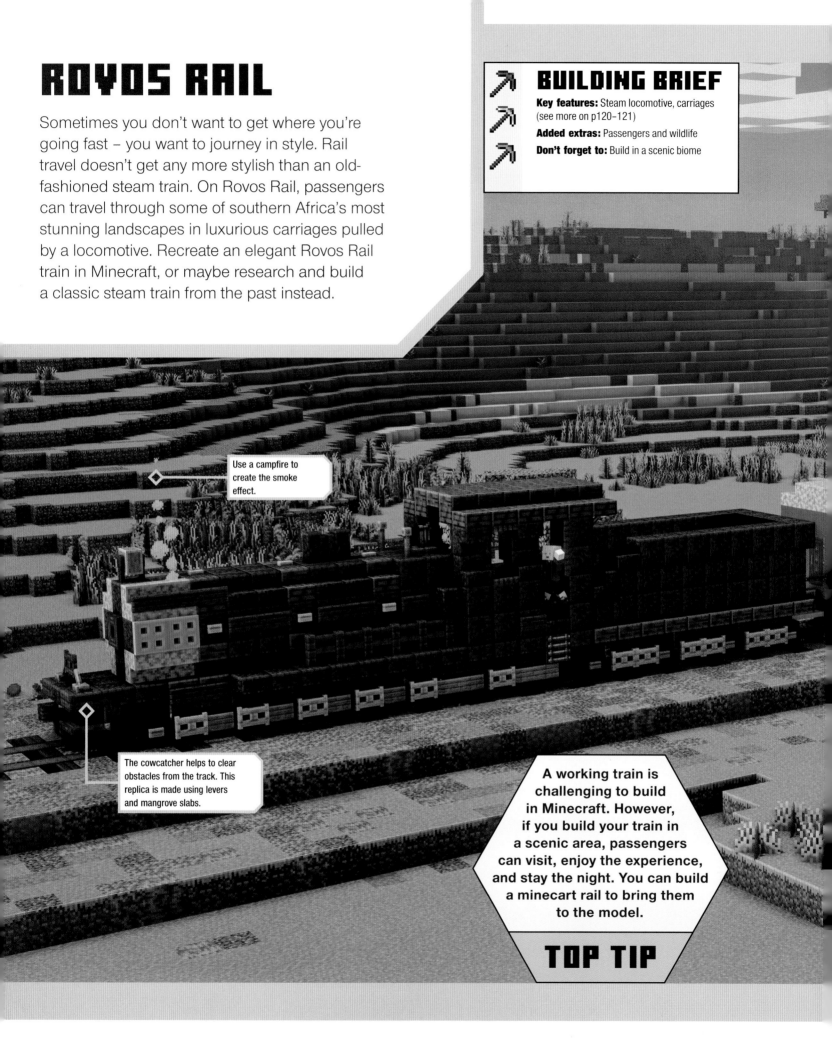

Use a campfire to create the smoke effect.

The cowcatcher helps to clear obstacles from the track. This replica is made using levers and mangrove slabs.

TOP TIP

A working train is challenging to build in Minecraft. However, if you build your train in a scenic area, passengers can visit, enjoy the experience, and stay the night. You can build a minecart rail to bring them to the model.

THE REAL DEAL

1 Rovos Rail's steam engines used to be powered by coal. They now run on oil, which is more efficient and less harmful to the environment.

2 Passengers can eat their meals in the luxury dining cars and spend the night on the train in suites with comfortable beds.

3 There is no Wi-Fi or television on Rovos Rail, so passengers can have an authentically old-fashioned travel experience.

BUILD HIGHLIGHTS

This Rovos Rail replica has been built in a savanna biome to match the wondrous landscapes seen in southern Africa. The flat, open area delivers spectacular views and the train is the perfect place to watch the glorious sunset.

Recreate the green colour of the carriages with green terracotta.

Add scaffolding windows to provide passengers with great views of the scenery.

COUPLINGS

Train carriages are joined together by mechanisms known as couplings. These Minecraft carriages are coupled with two grindstones and iron trapdoors. For safety, two chain handrails also link the carriages.

VIEWING BALCONY

Rovos Rail is as much about the journey as the destination, so it has viewing platforms to watch the scenery. This Minecraft version is made of warped trapdoors and fences and allows players to look out over the savanna biome.

BEST BLOCKS

This locomotive has 36 carriages behind it. You'll need lots of green terracotta and diorite for the carriages, and plenty of grindstones and iron trapdoors for the couplings.

GREEN TERRACOTTA

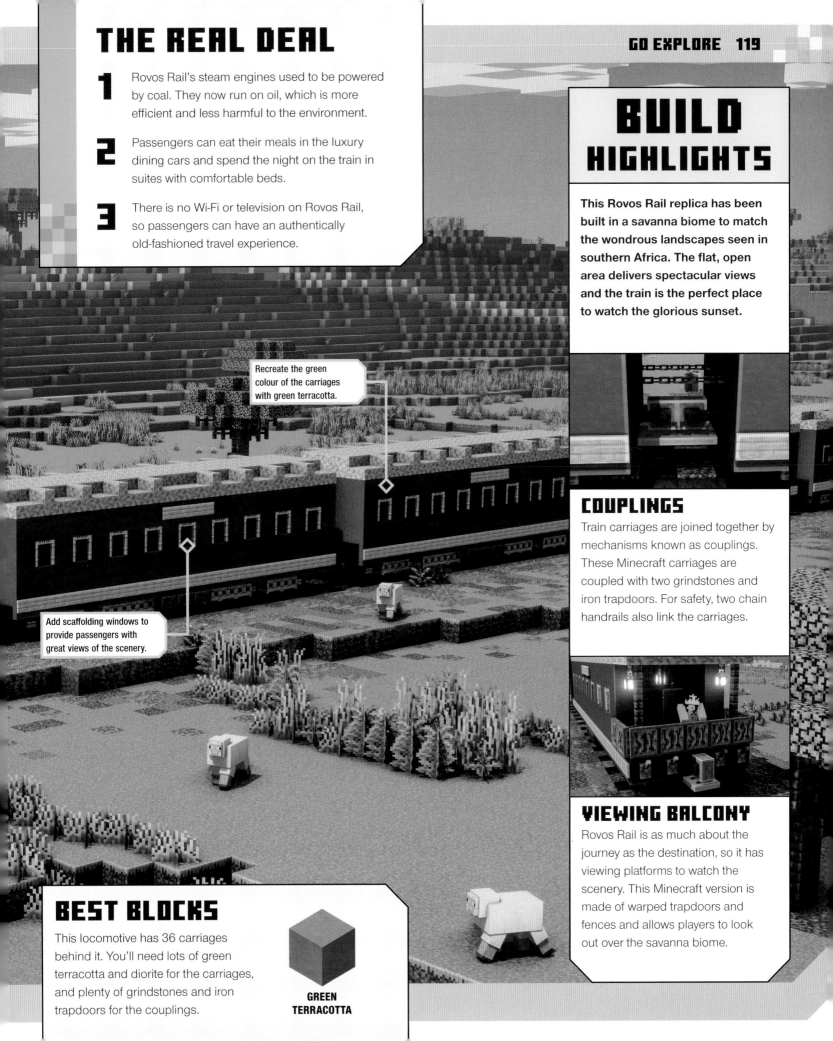

ROVOS RAIL: ALL ABOARD!

Rovos Rail is the pinnacle of leisurely rail transport. In the past, the classic steam locomotive had 36 luxurious carriages and carried a maximum of 72 passengers, in comfort and style. On board the train today you'll find find dining carriages, lavish accommodation carriages, and lounge carriages. What special activities will you include for your passengers in your Minecraft version? Remember, technology is restricted!

OIL LOCOMOTIVE

In a real oil-run steam engine, the engine driver burns oil to heat water. The hot water then turns into steam, which powers the engines and turns the wheels. Place a campfire in your locomotive's engine room to recreate the steam that jets out of the engine.

ENGINE ROOM

This Minecraft replica has recreated the Rovos Rail engine room using blast furnaces, levers, a campfire, and a brewing stand.

The body of the train uses polished deepslate block variants.

Mangrove signs and fences add red detailing to the engine design.

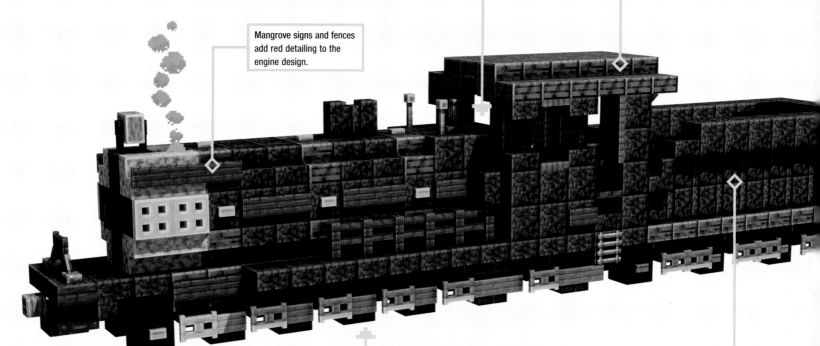

WHEELS

This Minecraft replica doesn't move, but that means you can get creative with the train wheels. These are made using black concrete with a button for a bolt. Birch fence gates fill the gaps in between.

Although coal is no longer used, the coal carriage is still attached to the Rovos Rail train.

CARRIAGES

Each Rovos Rail carriage is specially designed to offer a luxurious and authentic journey for its passengers. These Minecraft versions are 21 blocks long, 6 blocks tall, and 5 blocks wide. What luxurious details will you add to your carriage?

BUILD TIP

To build all the carriages of a Rovos Rail train, you will need to find a big, open space. Each carriage is 21 blocks long. For all 36 carriages, you'll need 756 blocks of tracks. Place rooted dirt and dark oak stairs in alternating blocks to count out the space, using anvils for rails.

Use green terracotta for the carriage's timeless grand exterior.

All kinds of passengers might take a train ride across Africa, from monarchs and presidents to traders and tourists.

You could add villagers to the carriage to act as passengers on a long journey.

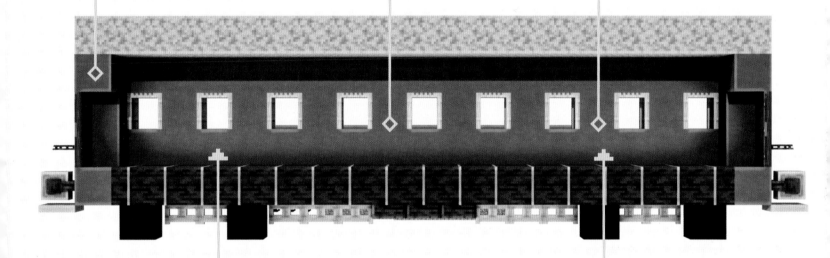

LOUNGE CAR

Provide your passengers with seats and a table using stair blocks and trapdoors. Add privacy walls with dark oak planks, coat hooks made from tripwire hooks, and a flowerpot for decoration.

DINING CAR

One of the best parts of a Rovos Rail trip is the food. Create an on-board fine-dining car with trapdoor tables and seating. Prepare a cake for afternoon tea.

ROCKET LAUNCH SITE

NASA's Space Launch System (SLS) is the biggest and most powerful rocket ever assembled. Part of the Artemis space programme, it is designed to launch the Orion spacecraft into space so that humans can explore further than ever before.

The SLS stands at a massive 98 m (322 ft) tall, so if you're up for a big building challenge, why not recreate it to scale in Minecraft? You'll need to find a large open space – a plains biome would be perfect – to create everything you need for your rocket launch site. It's time to get working on your very own SLS.

BUILDING BRIEF

Key features: SLS rocket, launchpad, control centre (see more on p124–125)

Added extras: Tracks, redstone, gardens

Don't forget to: Clear a large safety area around the rocket

BEST BLOCKS

Rocket launch sites require a flat ground surface and for structures to be made of strong, sturdy materials. This build uses lots of stone for the surface, and deepslate variants give the launch tower an industrial look.

DEEPSLATE BRICKS

ANDESITE

THE REAL DEAL

1 The SLS is equipped with two solid rocket boosters (SRBs), which each burn 6 tonnes (6.6 tons) of solid propellant per second to ignite the rocket's fuel.

2 In 2022, the SLS launched an uncrewed Orion into space, where it orbited the Moon.

3 Its next mission will take a crew of four astronauts around the Moon. NASA plans to use what it learns from these missions to create a lunar base – and to eventually send the first astronauts to Mars.

BUILD HIGHLIGHTS

While the rocket is undoubtedly the star of this build, it needs a launchpad to position it and prepare it for lift-off.

SECURING THE ROCKET

The rocket is transported to the launchpad for fuelling before lift-off. Add redstone-powered trapdoors to mechanical arms to grip your Minecraft rocket to the launchpad. To open and close the trapdoor, simply connect the trapdoor to a lever using redstone dust.

The main body of the Minecraft Orion spacecraft is made from calcite.

LAUNCH TOWER

Engineers perform maintenance and repairs until the engines are fired for lift-off. The launch tower at the rocket's side has a staircase that allows engineers access to every part of the rocket. Use lots of different deepslate block variants to create your Minecraft launch tower.

The Minecraft SLS rocket uses stripped acacia logs and calcite.

The launchpad has caterpillar tracks in case it needs to move. Use dispensers, polished deepslate, and deepslate brick stairs to recreate these.

Hot, fiery fumes erupt out of the base on lift-off. This effect is created with glowstone and glass blocks.

LOOK CLOSER

Rocket launches produce a huge amount of smoke. Pack the area around the base of your rocket with billowing smoke effects, using a mix of glass and cobwebs.

ROCKET LAUNCH SITE: COMPONENTS

The SLS needs huge engines and rocket boosters, as well as the help of experts in the mission control centre (and beyond), to blast the Orion spacecraft into space safely. You can use the blocks below for your SLS and control centre, or change things to suit your own style.

CONTROL ROOM

Create a busy, high-tech control centre with desks made from stairs and a slab. The computer screens are a pressure plate and a trapdoor and the chairs are made using stairs and signs. Levers are used as switches and controllers.

MISSION CONTROL

From launch to landing, all spaceflights are carefully overseen by mission control centres. Teams of flight controllers, engineers, and support staff work here. This two-storey Minecraft control centre stands on an intricate network of redstone dust that carries redstone signals to the working mechanisms on the SLS rocket stand, such as its mechanical arms.

Grey stained glass blocks allow the scientists and engineers to see the rocket.

Recreate the exhaust vents using four minecart rails.

Scientists rely on their eyes as well as their instruments, so include windows overlooking your rocket. Place two layers of glass blocks to help keep players safe when the rocket lifts off.

Use tough blocks, such as stone, cobblestone, and andesite for a building like this.

BUILD TIP

If you want to recreate this mission control centre exactly, here's how it stacks up: the main building is 36 blocks wide, 19 blocks deep, and 11 blocks tall. The smaller entrance is 48 blocks wide, 16 blocks deep, and 7 blocks tall.

REPEATERS

At this distance from the SLS rocket, the redstone dust needs redstone repeaters to boost the signal. Place a redstone repeater every 15 blocks to maintain the signal.

PARTS OF THE SLS

It takes incredible engineering and technology skills to build something capable of blasting off into space. In order to take the Orion spacecraft into space, the SLS's core carries huge tanks of liquid hydrogen and liquid oxygen propellant, which are burnt together in four engines at the base. Two solid rocket fuel boosters add even more thrust.

ORION

Orion is the exploration spacecraft that the SLS needs to launch. Create a 15-block-tall, 3x3 wide spacecraft using diorite walls, calcite, and birch fence gates.

Build the conical tips of the boosters with calcite blocks and diorite walls.

SLS ROCKET

The SLS rocket is designed to launch its payload (Orion) into space. Recreate the colours of the rocket with acacia and exposed cut copper. This version is 57 blocks tall (excluding the Orion spacecraft) and it measures 7x7 blocks wide.

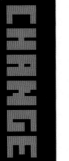

CHANGE IT!

NASA has designed more than a dozen unique rockets to take humans to outer space. You can research and then recreate any of these in Minecraft. Try building the *Titan III* or *Saturn V*. What blocks will you use?

ROCKET BOOSTERS

Two massive rocket boosters burn solid fuel, just like a firework does, which helps propel the SLS into space. These 42-block-tall Minecraft boosters are made from calcite with iron trapdoors.

Reinforce your build with iron trapdoors along the calcite boosters.

MARS, THE RED PLANET

Minecraft worlds are huge so there is plenty of space to recreate at least one of the planets in our solar system. Mars is a good choice for a build, with its distinctive orangey-red colour. The fourth planet from the Sun, Earth's neighbour gets its colour from the oxidized iron (rust) in its sand and rocks. You could choose any of a number of Minecraft blocks to recreate this colour, such as terracotta or red sandstone.

BUILDING BRIEF

Key features: A big sphere made of red and brown coloured blocks

Added extras: Polar ice caps, craters, dunes

Don't forget to: Think about how to make the perfect pitch-black, space-like background

THE REAL DEAL

1 Mars is the second smallest planet in our solar system, after Mercury. It's about half the size of Earth, and much colder.

2 You could jump about three times higher on Mars than on Earth because the planet's gravity (the force that pulls us down) is not as strong.

3 Mars could be suitable for humans to live on. NASA hopes to send astronauts on the first mission to Mars in the 2030s.

For a different surrounding, travel to the End dimension and find a pitch-black void to build your planet in.

Complete your intergalactic Mars scene by adding a space background. Use black concrete to recreate the dark night sky and add lanterns to represent distant stars.

TOP TIP

BEST BLOCKS

Mix red blocks with orange and brown blocks to create Mars' bumpy surface. This build is primarily made of red, orange, and brown terracotta. Wool blocks add texture, too.

RED TERRACOTTA

ORANGE TERRACOTTA

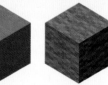
BROWN WOOL

Add white terracotta and white concrete on Mars' north pole to look like snow.

Mars' surface is full of craters, valleys, and dunes. It even has polar ice caps.

Using a mix of different coloured blocks adds texture and variety to the planet's surface.

Give your Mars rover a friendly face with a skeleton skull.

Place sea pickles and buttons to make your rover look high-tech.

ROBOT ROVER

The real Mars is inhabited by robots! These robots are stationary landers and wheeled rovers, which are deployed to study Mars up close. This friendly-looking rover has been made with mob skull wheels and a diorite wall arm, and it uses observers and grindstones for its machinery.

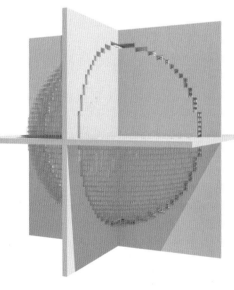

BUILD A SPHERE

Building a huge sphere can be tricky. The best way is to start with a skeleton shape. Create an outline of a big box and split it into four quadrants. Place one block in the corner of one quadrant and continue to place more blocks in a zig-zag formation until it creates a round shape reaching the far corner. Repeat this until you have completed one-quarter of the sphere, then repeat three times to complete the sphere.

INTERNATIONAL SPACE STATION

Travelling into space used to be a short adventure, with flights lasting a few days at most. Now, thanks to the International Space Station (ISS) you can actually live there! Since 2000, crews of six astronauts at a time have been able to spend months on board, studying space. You can embark on an interstellar adventure in Minecraft by building your own version of the ISS base.

BUILDING BRIEF

Key features: Rows of daylight sensors that power redstone, modules for living quarters (see more on p132–133), docking port

Added extras: An elytra landing room for visitors

Don't forget to: Bring supplies up to the ISS

Build a small cargo spacecraft to deliver supplies to the ISS.

Building a space station can be risky. It's a long way down! The best way to avoid fall damage in Survival mode is to land in water, so place a few water sources on the ground in case you misstep.

TOP TIP

The ISS gets regular deliveries of food, fuel, and replacement parts from Earth. It has a robotic arm to unload supplies.

THE REAL DEAL

1 Work began on the ISS in 1998 and it was finished in 2011. Over 260 astronauts from at least 20 countries have visited and worked on the ISS.

2 The ISS is the biggest artificial object to orbit the Earth. It is as big as a football pitch and can often be seen in the night sky.

3 The ISS travels very quickly, at about 8 km (5 miles) per second. It orbits the Earth once every 90 minutes. That's 16 times a day.

BUILD HIGHLIGHTS

Powering the ISS takes lots of energy. Thankfully, it has a source of renewable energy all around it – sunlight. A small spacecraft for delivering supplies is essential, too.

Daylight detectors

SOLAR POWER

Rows of solar panels on long arms (known as solar arrays) capture sunlight and turn it into electricity to meet the ISS's basic needs. Use dried kelp blocks to make solar arrays, and add daylight detectors to the middle and ends.

Add modules for living quarters, storage, and laboratories.

The green-lined look of the dried kelp blocks makes authentic-looking solar panels.

Space craft dock at these landing ports.

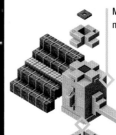

Main body is mostly made from stone.

Use stone slabs and stone stairs to connect the solar panels.

Build the cargo ship using the same blocks as the ISS.

CARGO SPACECRAFT

In the real world, unpiloted robotic spacecraft deliver supplies to the ISS. Recreate this cargo delivery spacecraft in Minecraft, and fill it with shulker boxes. Each box can store 27 stacks of items, which means you could transport up to 13,824 cookies!

BEST BLOCKS

Materials for the ISS were transported from Earth by rocket, so they had to be light. This build uses blocks that represent light materials, such as dried kelp blocks and iron bars.

DRIED KELP BLOCKS

IRON BARS

ISS: INTERIOR

The interior of the ISS is made up of airtight chambers known as modules where astronauts eat, sleep, and study. There's even a gym to help them stay fit and strong. This Minecraft build includes a tiny farm. Add extra modules with all the equipment you think you might need. How about an enchanting table and brewing stands for discovering Minecraft's secrets? Use your imagination!

SCIENCE PLATFORM

Create a room with lots of dials to replicate the station's support systems. Place compasses on the walls to mimic monitors tracking levels of atmospheric pressure and radiation.

LANDING PORT

For fun, try to reach the station in Survival mode. Players can fly using an elytra and fireworks. They can enter the station via this narrow mangrove trapdoor entrance, and then crawl through the tunnel and into the station.

BUILD TIP

This build is set in the Overworld, which is ideal for a large-scale model like the ISS. Alternatively, for a darker, more void-like appearance you could travel to the End and build it there. Find an open space in the void to get started.

FARM

Build a compact farm to keep passengers fed. Add tech to your farm with a lever and piston, and add your favourite crop. Pull the lever to harvest your crop, then retill the soil and plant a new seed for the next player.

POLAR RESEARCH SHIP

Almost 80 percent of the ocean has never been seen by humans. We know a little bit about what's out there, such as deep trenches, underwater volcanoes, and amazing animals, but we need to find out more. Research ships, like the RRS *Sir David Attenborough*, are built for ocean exploration and equipped with all the latest technology to collect information. They are known as "icebreakers" because they are tough enough to navigate through the the icy oceans near the North and South Poles. Head to a frozen ocean biome and get started on your own polar ship.

BUILDING BRIEF

Key features: Research ship, icebergs

Added extras: Autonomous underwater vehicle, map

Don't forget to: Pack a variety of rations to ensure your hunger saturation levels don't drop

Add a smooth quartz block to recreate the satellite communications that allow the crew to stay in touch with the mainland.

Build your ship near naturally generated icebergs in frozen oceans and deep frozen oceans.

The "H" on this helideck can be seen from far away. It's made from green and white carpet.

Use mangrove trapdoors to shape the bow of the ship.

BEST BLOCKS

The RRS *Sir David Attenborough*'s red colours make it stand out from the icy blue ocean. This build uses red concrete and mangrove slabs, trapdoors, and stairs.

RED CONCRETE

MANGROVE SLAB

THE REAL DEAL

1 The UK's RRS (Royal Research Ship) *Sir David Attenborough* is the most advanced ocean research vessel. It is equipped to spend 60 days at sea with 90 crew and scientists on board.

2 The public were asked to name the vessel. Boaty McBoatface was the popular choice, but the builders decided to honour the naturalist Sir David Attenborough instead.

3 The name Boaty McBoatface was given to the ship's lead deep-sea submersible.

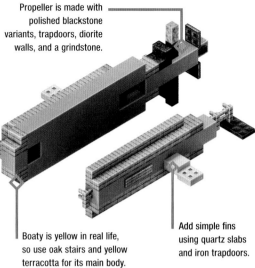

Propeller is made with polished blackstone variants, trapdoors, diorite walls, and a grindstone.

Boaty is yellow in real life, so use oak stairs and yellow terracotta for its main body.

Add simple fins using quartz slabs and iron trapdoors.

A cargo crane at the stern (rear) is made with a grindstone hook.

Iron bars make a great safety rail around the deck.

BOATY MCBOATFACE

Boaty McBoatface is the ship's lead AUV (autonomous underwater vehicle). AUVs can explore the deepest parts of the ocean without a crew. Boaty can be launched to depths of up to 6,000 m (19,685 ft) and can travel for up to 1,000 km (620 miles). It can even travel under ice! This Minecraft model is 15 blocks long and 7 blocks wide, with a fin on both sides and a propeller at the back.

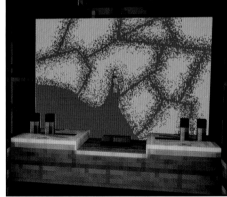

MAP MAKING

You can explore and record your ocean's world by using maps and creating a big map board. Create a 3x2 block surface and place item frames on the blocks. When you've completed your map, place it into the frame. Think about what else you can put in the cabins. Adding redstone elements will make your lab look high-tech.

Despite the freezing conditions, many mobs can be found in cold biomes. Not all of them are dangerous, but polar bears can become hostile – especially if you approach their babies.

TOP TIP

BROOKLYN BRIDGE

The Brooklyn Bridge is an iconic landmark in New York City, USA. Completed in 1883, it was the largest suspension bridge in the world for 20 years and the first to be built from steel. The bridge took 600 workers 14 years to build. Why not build a bridge in Minecraft to connect two islands? Afterwards, you could take a boat ride under it and admire the beautiful view – and your incredible building skills.

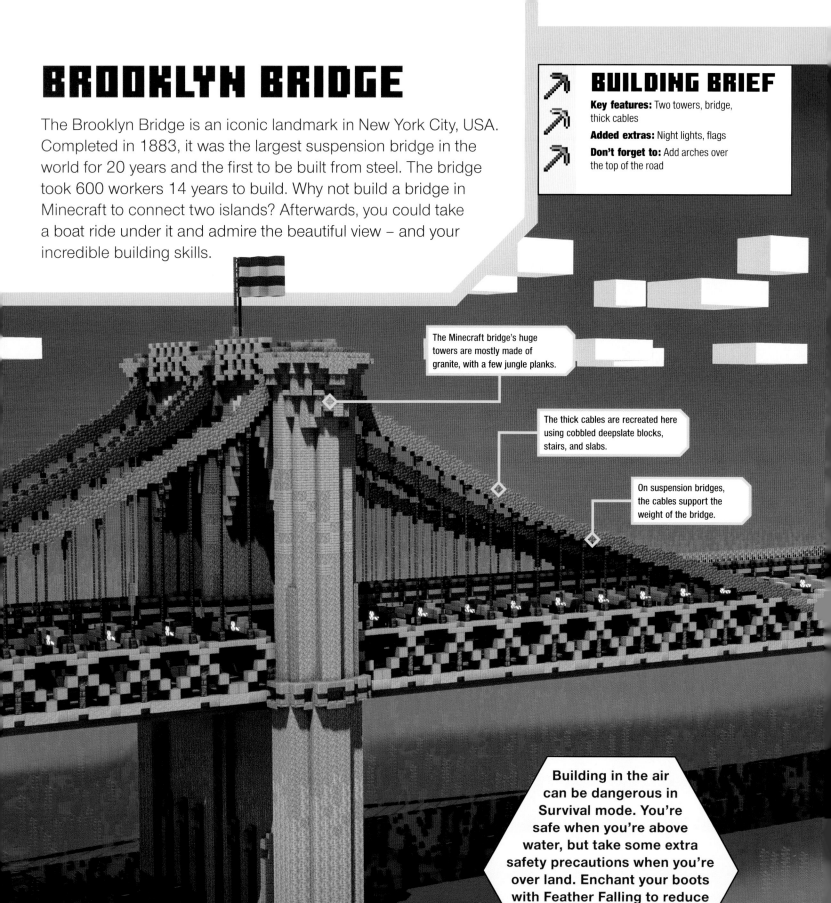

The Minecraft bridge's huge towers are mostly made of granite, with a few jungle planks.

The thick cables are recreated here using cobbled deepslate blocks, stairs, and slabs.

On suspension bridges, the cables support the weight of the bridge.

Building in the air can be dangerous in Survival mode. You're safe when you're above water, but take some extra safety precautions when you're over land. Enchant your boots with Feather Falling to reduce possible fall damage.

TOP TIP

THE REAL DEAL

1 The Brooklyn Bridge crosses the East River, connecting the boroughs of Brooklyn and Manhattan.

2 Some people worried that the Brooklyn Bridge wasn't safe. The builders invited the showman PT Barnum to cross it with 21 elephants to prove that it was steady!

3 Despite being credited as a suspension bridge, the Brooklyn Bridge is technically a "cable-stayed" bridge. The brick towers are attached by super strong cables directly to the deck of the bridge.

ROAD ARCHES

New York is known as the city that never sleeps. But if you don't sleep in Minecraft, phantoms start to spawn. To help keep visitors safe in Survival mode, smooth stone slab arches have been added to this build to prevent phantoms from swooping down on players. The sides of the bridge are also lined with deepslate and stone block variants to prevent players from falling off.

The bridge is anchored by two tall towers.

Flags can be made from dyed wool and spruce fence posts.

Hold your bridge's cables in place with hanger ropes made of chains and walls.

NIGHT LIGHTS

This model has an elegant solution to keeping a build lit up at night: daylight detectors and redstone lamps. Place the daylight detectors and redstone lamps on the bridge arches. You can then set the daylight detector to "inverted" so that it lights up at night instead of during the day.

BEST BLOCKS

Many blocks are suitable for bridges, like granite and cobbled deepslate. For this build though, it is essential to create chains. They can be crafted from two iron nuggets and an iron ingot.

GRANITE

COBBLED DEEPSLATE

THE GRAND BAZAAR

The Grand Bazaar in Istanbul was once the busy trading centre of the Ottoman Empire. It was founded by Sultan Mehmed II in 1461. Today, the bazaar features everything a trading hub needs: shopfronts, storehouses, banks, and even accommodation and schools. Every world needs a trade centre, whether that's to trade with other players or villagers. What will you sell in your shop?

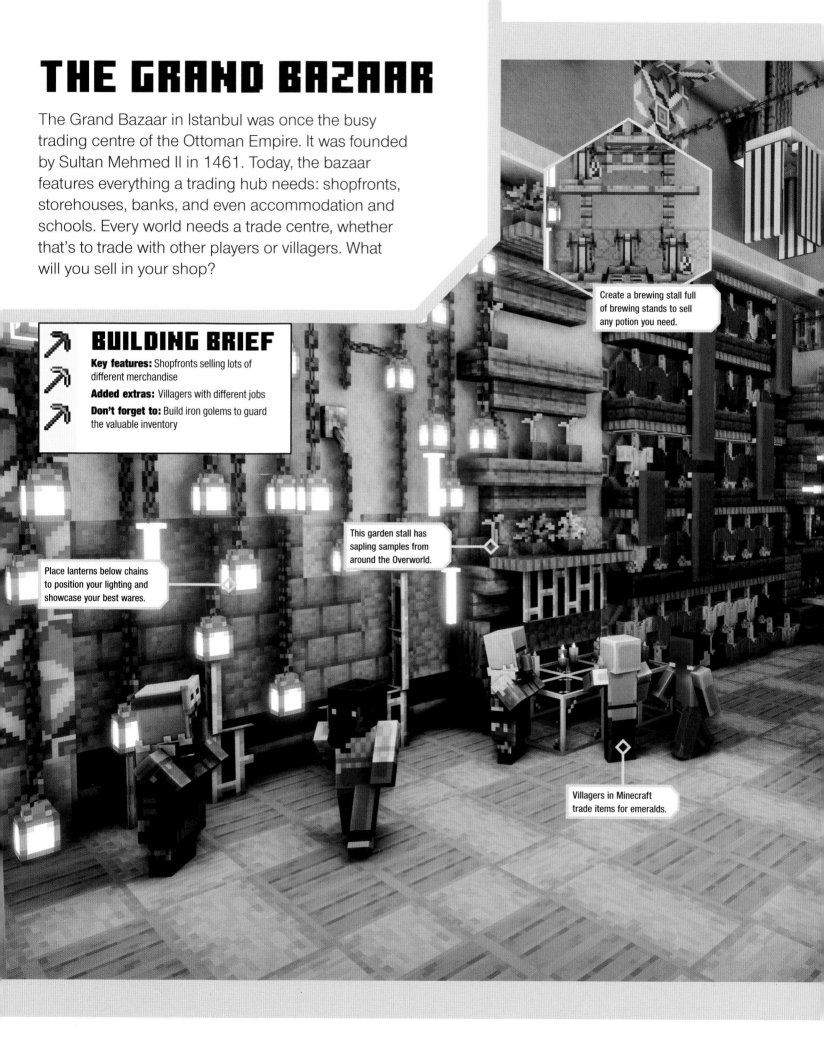

Create a brewing stall full of brewing stands to sell any potion you need.

BUILDING BRIEF

Key features: Shopfronts selling lots of different merchandise

Added extras: Villagers with different jobs

Don't forget to: Build iron golems to guard the valuable inventory

This garden stall has sapling samples from around the Overworld.

Place lanterns below chains to position your lighting and showcase your best wares.

Villagers in Minecraft trade items for emeralds.

THE REAL DEAL

1 The Grand Bazaar has been destroyed by fires and earthquakes over the centuries. But it has been rebuilt, even grander, every time.

2 The trade hub is one of the biggest buildings in the world. It has a network of 61 streets covering an area the size of around 43 football pitches and housing over 4,500 shops.

3 Every day, more than 400,000 shoppers visit the Grand Bazaar to check out the wares.

EYE-CATCHING DISPLAYS

The bazaar has narrow streets. Make the most of your shop space with a well-designed shopfront. Place rows of iron bars to hang banners, or create shelves with trapdoors and slabs. You can add iron bars for added security. Players can still see what you have on offer behind them.

Adding chains takes little space and provides a surface to hang items like banners overhead.

Villagers have five trade levels. You can see which trade level they are by looking at their belt. You'll see stone for novice, iron for apprentice, gold for journeyman, emerald for expert, and diamond for master.

TOP TIP

Make a textured floor using beehives.

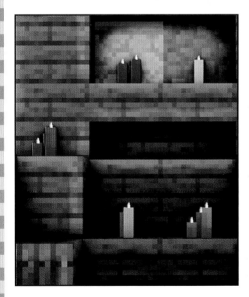

FANCY LIGHTING

Candles are a fun way to add soft lighting to the bazaar. You can craft up to 16 colours of candles using honeycomb, string, and dye. Use flint and steel to light the candles. Like sea pickles, candles can be placed in groups of one to four. The more candles you place, the brighter the light in your bazaar.

BEST BLOCKS

Use plenty of brown blocks, such as packed mud and mud bricks, with glazed terracotta for touches of colour. Chains are useful for hanging colourful items from the ceiling, too.

MUD BRICKS

GLAZED TERRACOTTA

CHÂTEAU DE CHENONCEAU

This magical 16th century château in the French countryside looks like it is floating on water. The Château de Chenonceau is built on arches that stretch across the Cher river in central France. Transport yourself back to a time when wild parties and lavish balls were held in this grand château. If you're a Minecrafter with a taste for the finer side of life, then this is the build for you. Create a mesmerizing castle of your own.

BUILDING BRIEF

Key features: Arches stretching across water, many windows

Added extras: Elegant rooms inside

Don't forget to: Build docks for visiting players

BUILD TIP

Not all masterpieces were impressive from the start. In fact, many had humble beginnings. This building was once an old watermill before being renovated into the world-famous château it is today. Do you have any old structures you can repurpose into an impressive new build?

Quartz bricks give this Minecraft castle a dazzling appearance in the sunlight.

BEST BLOCKS

Quartz variants are the perfect materials for a grand castle like this. Use quartz bricks, quartz pillars, and blocks of quartz. If you're playing in Survival mode, finding quartz will require a trip to the Nether.

QUARTZ

THE REAL DEAL

1 The Château de Chenonceau has a long history. Built as a watermill, it spent time as an unofficial royal court, and has also been used as a military hospital.

2 Diane de Poitiers held court here as queen of France in all but name in 1547–1559. She was King Henry II's royal mistress and adviser.

3 It is known as the "Ladies' Castle" because five women, including Diane de Poitiers, played a major role in its construction and preservation.

Create a narrow bridge using open trapdoors for barriers.

Make perfect chimney caps with skeleton skulls.

Use iron trapdoors, diorite walls, and End rods to build grand windows.

Some of the windows in this build appear to be covered with gold – but they're actually made from scaffolding!

GRAND ENTRANCE

Access to the château is across a bridge and through the grand entrance. In Minecraft, doors are only 2 blocks tall. This build uses the very similar-looking dark oak trapdoors and dark oak door to create a magnificent entrance that's more than twice as large.

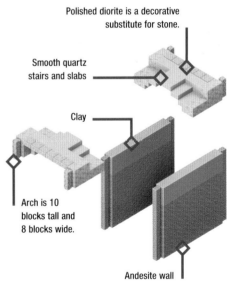

Polished diorite is a decorative substitute for stone.

Smooth quartz stairs and slabs

Clay

Arch is 10 blocks tall and 8 blocks wide.

Andesite wall

BUILD AN ARCH

These impressive arches ensure the river can flow unhindered. The arch design is super simple and can be used for many purposes. You could also use arches inside, for rooms such as hallways.

HOT-AIR BALLOON

Did you know that before planes were invented, the best way to fly was by hot-air balloon? Nearly 250 years ago, the world's first hot-air balloon flight took off carrying a cockerel, a sheep, and a duck. That same year, the first humans flew, too. Although planes have long since overtaken hot-air balloons as humans' favourite way to fly, balloons are still used for recreation and sport. You can try building a hot-air balloon in Minecraft. Although it won't actually fly anywhere, it'll be a fantastic piece of engineering and will make your skyline look spectacular.

BUILDING BRIEF

Key features: Large balloon, basket for passengers

Added extras: Colourful wool blocks

Don't forget to: Build a campfire to represent the hot-air balloon's burner

The balloon part is also called an envelope.

THE REAL DEAL

1 Hot-air balloons fly by becoming lighter than air. Air inside the hot-air balloon is heated. As it gets hotter, it becomes less dense and floats upwards, carrying the balloon up into the sky.

2 The first hot-air balloon flight with humans took place on November 21, 1783 in Paris. The balloon was made of paper and silk.

3 The balloon got about 152 m (500 ft) high and travelled about 9 km (5.5 miles).

LOOK CLOSER

Did you know that you can actually fly in Survival mode? Travel to the End dimension, defeat the Ender Dragon, and search for an End ship where you will find an elytra. This magical cape will allow you to glide through the air. Store one on board your hot-air balloon, like a lifejacket for the skies.

BEST BLOCKS

These huge, colourful balloons need to use every wool block available. Wool is the perfect material because it can be dyed any colour you like.

MAGENTA WOOL   ORANGE WOOL

Use lots of different colours of wool blocks to make your balloon stand out in the sky.

Hot-air balloons have a small valve at the top to deflate them. Use a dark oak trapdoor to recreate this in Minecraft.

Draped sides add extra decoration to the Minecraft balloons.

Passengers, known as balloonists, ride in a basket.

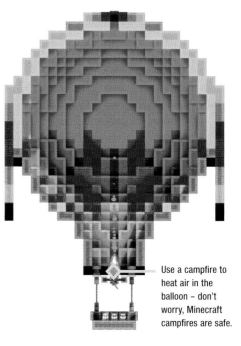

Use a campfire to heat air in the balloon – don't worry, Minecraft campfires are safe.

THE BALLOON

Most hot-air balloons are dome-shaped like this one. (See tips for how to build a sphere on p127.) But you can be creative and make your balloon any shape you like. Maybe yours will look like a creeper head or a sheep! Once you have built your balloon shape, decorate the outside with colourful wool blocks to create a unique design.

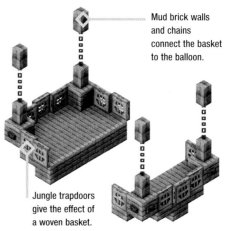

Mud brick walls and chains connect the basket to the balloon.

Jungle trapdoors give the effect of a woven basket.

BALLOONIST BASKET

Passengers can be carried around in hanging baskets like this one. This build uses jungle planks and slabs for the basket, and then mud brick walls and chains to attach it to the balloon. Add extra basket details with buttons.

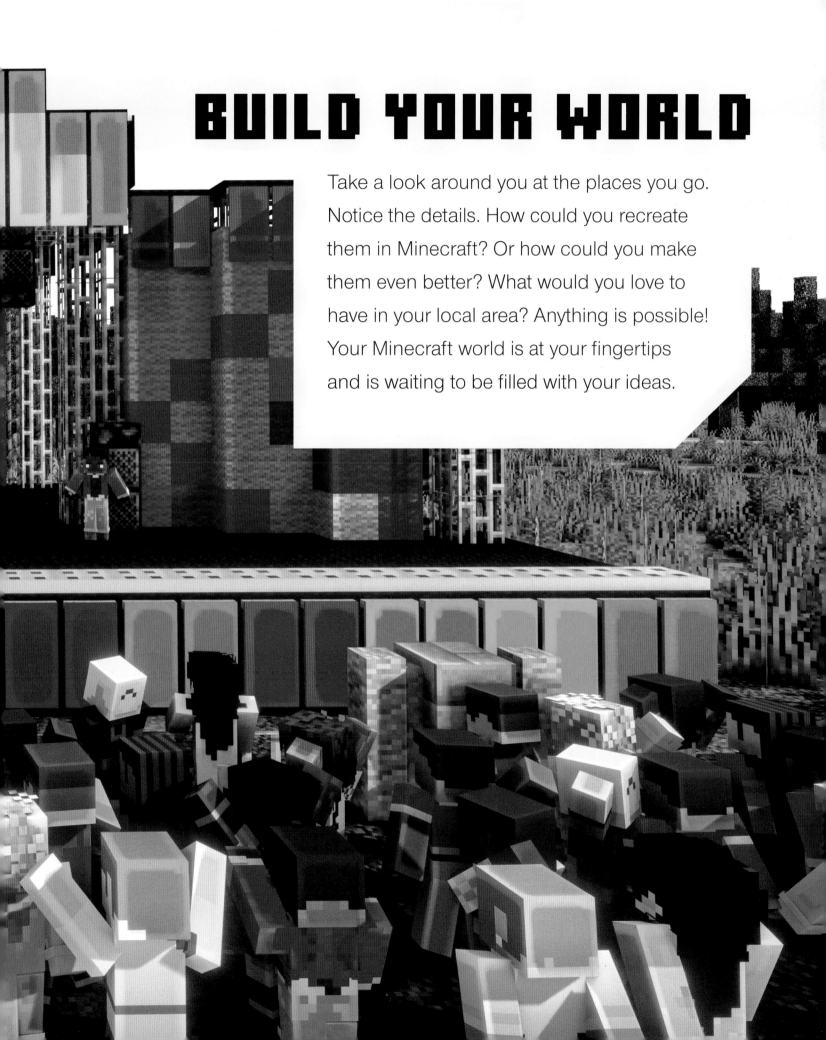

BUILD YOUR WORLD

Take a look around you at the places you go. Notice the details. How could you recreate them in Minecraft? Or how could you make them even better? What would you love to have in your local area? Anything is possible! Your Minecraft world is at your fingertips and is waiting to be filled with your ideas.

MICRO CITY

There's a really easy way to build a sprawling Minecraft city in record time – make it miniature. It's also a great way to explore your creative side. With some imaginative thinking and clever planning, you can create roads, shops, houses, and more to make a bustling (but tiny) town or city. Think of different ways you can use regular blocks to bring your town to life with interesting features and realistic details. It's time to think big but build small.

A lime concrete smokestack blends in with the surrounding greenery.

Use moss and leaves to create custom foliage for your city.

Build a kids' playground using iron bars and scaffolding.

Building in miniature is so satisfyingly simple. You can make single-block structures and then add windows. For high-rise buildings, just add a few more blocks to make the structures taller. Using lots of different slabs will make your simple city bright and colourful.

LOOK CLOSER

THE REAL DEAL

Model villages are always built to scale. Some can be as small as 1:76 – that means the model is 76 times smaller than the real thing. The world's largest miniature village is Miniatur Wunderland in Hamburg, Germany. It has more than 4,000 buildings. Meanwhile, the world's oldest model village is Bekonscot Model Village & Railway in the UK. It opened in 1929 and has had more than 15 million visitors.

RENEWABLE ENERGY

Future-proof your city by building it a clean, renewable energy source. In the real world, wind turbines can turn one of Earth's natural resources, wind, into electricity to power a city. Add tiny turbines to your Minecraft build using diorite walls, End rods, iron trapdoors, and skeleton skulls.

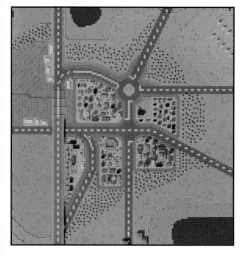

CITY PLANNING

Before you start building, take some time to plan your city. Decide on its shape and style, and think about where everything should go. You could start by planning the roads and transport links. You could also divide your city into different sections. This build has a residential area and a farming area. What else might you include?

Slabs are perfect for creating colourful roofs.

Use terracotta to make eye-catching pavements or andesite for smaller paths.

Add buttons to make perfect little windows.

BEST BLOCKS

Although it's a miniature city, you can still use lots of different blocks. This build uses many of the white blocks in the game, such as snow, calcite, bone, wool, and quartz to create a Mediterranean-style town.

SMOOTH QUARTZ

BONE BLOCKS

NATURAL HISTORY MUSEUM

There are more than 100,000 museums on Earth, built to celebrate and preserve objects from history, works of art and anything else that humans find fascinating. This Minecraft Natural History Museum has an impressive dinosaur skeleton plus lots of other interesting artefacts. Build your own museum in Minecraft to display the objects you find on your adventures. What treasures have you uncovered?

Use blocks like smooth quartz, bone blocks, and diorite walls to create this Triceratops model.

Create a chandelier using a hopper, a mud brick block, jungle fences, and torches.

Keep visitors from climbing on the fossils with an iron bar fence.

There are many ways to create displays in Minecraft. Frames are perfect for smaller objects, while armour stands are ideal for larger equipment. Any blocks can also be placed in custom-designed cabinets.

TOP TIP

This tiled floor is made using polished andesite and basalt.

THE REAL DEAL

Museums come in all shapes and sizes. In New York, the Treasures in the Trash exhibition celebrates the things that people throw away, while in the UK there are museums dedicated to lawnmowers and pencils. Beijing, China, has the Tap Water Museum, and New Delhi, India, has a museum dedicated to toilets!

This display is 3 blocks deep. The glass blocks showcase the plant leaves, while sea lanterns illuminate from behind.

Add a lectern with a book to display item information.

BUILD HIGHLIGHTS

Museums are inspiring places to visit. Think about the kind of building that could show off your treasures. It might be a sleek, modern museum or one that looks old and full of history. Decide how visitors will explore your museum, what should go where, and how objects should be displayed.

DISPLAYS

Use blocks from throughout Minecraft to create displays for your museum. This traditional two-handled vase is built with mud bricks and jungle trapdoors.

STUNNING DETAILS

This Minecraft museum features a huge domed glass ceiling that lets in lots of light during the day. To create your own, start by building support arches and then fill the space between them with glass blocks.

BEST BLOCKS

A museum can be made with any of your favourite blocks – this build uses sandstone. The most important parts, however, are your display cabinets. Trapdoors and glass panes work really well for these.

TRAPDOOR

GLASS PANE

NATURAL HISTORY MUSEUM: MAKING THE EXHIBITS

After building the museum, you have to think about what your treasures might be and how best to show them off and keep them safe. Large artefacts from ancient times can be free-standing, while delicate items from the natural world are best protected in sturdy display cases. Whatever you decide to dedicate your museum to, make sure you have an exciting, audience-drawing centrepiece on display for all the visitors to see.

BUILD TIP

Think about the size of your museum build, and make sure that there's enough room to fit in all your treasures as well as space for visitors to admire them. This museum has 13-block-tall walls. That's plenty of space for artefacts and the fancy chandelier lighting above them.

Make a cabinet that is 5 blocks tall, 5 blocks wide (with trapdoors), and 3 blocks deep.

ARTEFACTS

Recreate incredible artefacts from around the world or make up your own treasures. This 6.5-block-tall andesite statue has a simple but effective body shape. Use other blocks or buttons to create details such as eyes and limbs.

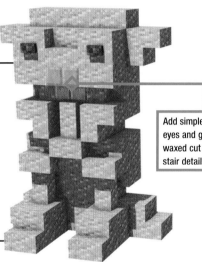

Add simple button eyes and green waxed cut copper stair details.

DISPLAY CASE

Visitors can look but not touch this beautiful collection of minerals, gems, and metals. Light grey stained glass and jungle trapdoors keep the raw amethyst, copper, iron, and gold safely locked away but easy to view. You can also save space by building the cabinet into the museum wall.

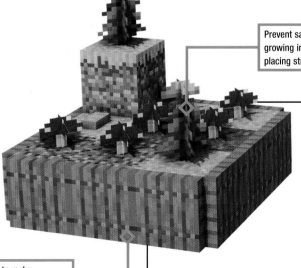

Prevent saplings from growing into trees by placing string above them.

MINIATURE GARDEN

Your exhibits don't have to be big. This miniature garden is dedicated to plants and fungi. You could also recreate a miniature early settlement or town. (See the Micro City on p144–145 for tips.)

Use trapdoors to make space-efficient borders and barriers to protect displays.

CENTREPIECE

Most museums have at least one extra-special exhibit – the one that draws in the crowds. This museum's centrepiece is a magnificent recreation of a Triceratops skeleton, mostly made of bone and quartz blocks.

CHANGE IT!

Your centrepiece can be anything: a different dinosaur, a statue, a painting, an object, or a sculpture. Imagine a museum dedicated to Minecraft itself. What might your awesome centrepiece be then?

Use diorite walls to add details like tusks and teeth.

Bone blocks make up the inner skeleton of the Triceratops.

READ ABOUT IT

Share all the amazing facts you know about dinosaurs with your visitors via an information stand. Write everything inside a book and place it on the stand.

Craft a book using one leather and three papers in a crafting table.

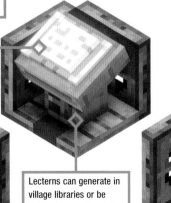

Add quartz stairs to create feet and other details. Stairs can be placed to add sharp edges or combined to create curves and angles.

Add jungle trapdoors to the sides of the lectern to create the information stand.

Lecterns can generate in village libraries or be built using wooden slabs and a bookshelf.

ROADWAYS

When our ancestors invented the wheel more than 6,000 years ago, it changed human society forever. Being able to travel longer distances allowed people to trade with each other and learn about different cultures. Today, transport allows us to stay connected, gives us access to vital services, and provides us with commodities from all over the globe. In Minecraft, whether you travel by foot, horse, or minecart, building highways will connect you to the rest of the Overworld.

BUILDING BRIEF

Key features: Raised highways, intersections
Added extras: Lights, signs
Don't forget to: Link the highway to your bases

CHANGE IT!

Change the roadways to fit your favourite travel style. If you're travelling by horse, add posts and leashes for stopping points. Hikers can always use a bed to rest for the night, and minecarters can install rails all along the roadways.

Add lighting on the road to prevent mobs from spawning at night.

Pillars keep the road off the ground so local plants and mobs are not disturbed.

BEST BLOCKS

In the real world, the best roadways are made of smooth, durable tarmac and asphalt. Recreate these materials in Minecraft by using similar-looking blocks such as cyan terracotta and andesite.

CYAN TERRACOTTA

ANDESITE

THE REAL DEAL

The longest road in the world is the Pan-American Highway. It's over 30,600 km (19,000 miles) long, and stretches from the north of Alaska all the way south through Mexico and Costa Rica to the southern tip of Argentina. If you drove around 500 km (300 miles) a day, it would take more than 61 days to travel the length of this road.

Build a 1-block-tall wall to keep the roads free from roaming mobs.

Add signs for road safety and to direct road users to local sights and facilities.

Two roads cross at this bridged intersection. One road continues above and the other below.

GO HIGH

Building in Minecraft will bring you across winding rivers and deep ravines, which can all cause problems. Luckily, you can work around anything with a simple trick: elevation. Raise the highway above the ground so that you can build over any obstacles. Building pillars ten blocks above the ground will allow your road to clear most obstacles.

SIGNPOSTS

Add signs to give travellers directions to nearby bases and to tell of upcoming amenities, like toilets and petrol stations. Signs can also provide warnings of dangers, such as nearby pillager outposts. Magenta glazed terracotta is perfect for arrows, or you can use frames for holding items. A frame with a mob head can warn of danger to come!

WATER PARK OBSTACLE COURSE

People have been enjoying wet, wild, and wonderful water park rides since the world's first water park opened in Orlando, Florida, in the 1970s. They are a great place to have fun with your friends and an awesome project to build in Minecraft. Let your imagination flow and create an obstacle course for your park. You can build your own features using water, honey, and slime.

Add slime to bounce higher – just high enough to make it across the course!

Start here!

Take a running jump to skip across the slab pads.

Watch your step! Touching the hot magma will burn your toes.

You're one slip away from a splash on the Stepping Stones.

The Pack-a-Punch works on a timed circuit to knock you into the water.

BEST BLOCKS

When building an obstacle course, the best blocks are the ones with special features. Honey is sticky, ice is slippery, and slime is bouncy. What else could you use?

HONEY   **BLUE ICE**

THE REAL DEAL

Water parks use a lot of water. Hundreds of thousands of litres of it! This may sound a bit wasteful, but modern water parks are capable of reusing as much as 97 percent of the water. The remaining three percent is lost to evaporation.

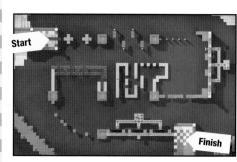

MAP

This obstacle course features nine unique features to test the mettle of any Minecrafter. You'll bounce, skip, jump, slide, run, and, if you're unlucky, swim before you reach the finishing line. Place a map by the starting line for players to prepare themselves for the challenge ahead.

Cling to the sticky wall as you make your way across.

The Stick-and-Slide uses the stickiest block in Minecraft – honey!

Take your time crossing the fence posts – these narrow platforms are tricky to land on.

Skate and hop your way to the net platform. Blue ice is slippery, so take it slow.

Hurry across the walkway.

Finish here!

Most of this course uses the special blocks, like ice and honey. But not all. You can use redstone to create some sneaky features too, like the piston in Pack-a-Punch. This uses a redstone clock circuit to keep the sticky pistons popping in and out to catch out players.

LOOK CLOSER

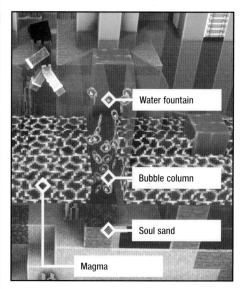

Water fountain

Bubble column

Soul sand

Magma

MAGMA MENACE

In the real world, slips and falls are the only risks you face in a water obstacle course. But this is Minecraft, so you can take it to the next level. To create this Magma Menace obstacle, place a block of soul sand with a "fountain" above it in between each magma platform. The soul sand will propel the player upwards via a bubble column. Players will have to skip, jump, or hop between each so they don't get toasted by the magma.

FOREST FIRE LOOKOUT

Look out – there's a thunderstorm coming. A forest biome is a dangerous place when thunder strikes. One small spark is all it takes to set it ablaze. This forest fire lookout, with its high vantage point, is ideal for keeping an eye out for forest fires and also for pillager patrols searching for villages to raid.

BUILDING BRIEF

Key features: Forest fire lookout tower, trees

Added extras: Firefighting equipment, a warning bell

Don't forget to: Include an infinite water supply

LOOK CLOSER

In real life, shovelling dirt over your campfire will help to put it out. Minecraft campfires don't need to be put out, but you can add a shovel to your build, along with a flint and steel ready for when you want to light it again. Then, relax by taking a seat on some chairs made of wooden stairs and trapdoors and enjoy the view.

This roof is made with blackstone block variants.

Add a lightning rod at the top of the tower to protect against lightning strikes.

Create a platform using trapdoors.

This narrow build only has room for spiral steps made using stair blocks.

THE REAL DEAL

Forest fires are a real danger. Ground temperatures can reach over 1,000°C (1,832°F)! There are thousands of watchtowers around the world staffed day and night as part of fire prevention programmes. Although very dangerous, wildfires can sometimes be beneficial. Burned vegetation returns nutrients to the soil, making it more fertile for future plants.

FIREBREAKS

Forest fires can spread wildly and rapidly. In the real world, firefighters use a special trick to stop the fire spreading: a firebreak. Firefighters rapidly knock down trees to create a gap in the forest so the fire cannot spread any further. To create an emergency firebreak in Survival mode, make sure you have Efficiency V enchanted axes or even TNT handy to remove trees and make a gap.

Build extra-tall trees, but make sure that the tower is even taller to give players a vantage point.

Noise travels far in open spaces. Add a bell near your tower to sound the alarm when you see smoke or when pillagers come raiding.

Fires will spread quickly in Minecraft. Areas with flammable blocks, such as forests, will always be at risk.

Water is perfect for extinguishing fires. Place three water sources next to each other to always have an infinite water supply to hand.

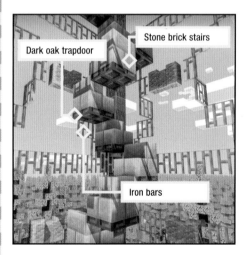

Dark oak trapdoor

Stone brick stairs

Iron bars

SPIRAL STAIRS

When the risk of fire makes ladders too dangerous to use and narrow structures make stairs difficult to fit, it's time to get creative with ways to climb. This build uses narrowly-placed stair blocks to create a vertical staircase in as small a space as possible. Be careful though – there's no handrail. Use scaffolding when building structures without floors. It gives you a space to stand while you build.

BEST BLOCKS

When you're building a forest fire lookout, it is important to include non-flammable materials. Use blocks like iron bars, polished andesite, and stone bricks to make your structure.

STONE BRICKS

IRON BARS

POLISHED ANDESITE

OUTDOOR CONCERT STAGE

Movies and TV shows are great, but there's nothing like the excitement of watching a live show, especially if it's outdoors. A concert stage can be used by musicians, comedians, dancers, and actors. Even the smallest towns and villages usually have somewhere for people to perform. You can build amazing stages in Minecraft, and even create your own music. Rock on!

THE REAL DEAL

Over 5,300 Minecraft players watched Minecraft's in-game Fire Festival concert in January 2019, featuring virtual performances from over 50 acts. More than 80,000 others joined in via the Fire Festival website and Discord server.

Customize your stage with banners and wool blocks in bright colours.

There are 16 different discs in Minecraft. Use a chest to store the discs.

In Minecraft, you can use note blocks to create a wide range of sounds. For a more complex instrument, try adding a pressure plate or button to send out a redstone signal and trigger the note blocks.

TOP TIP

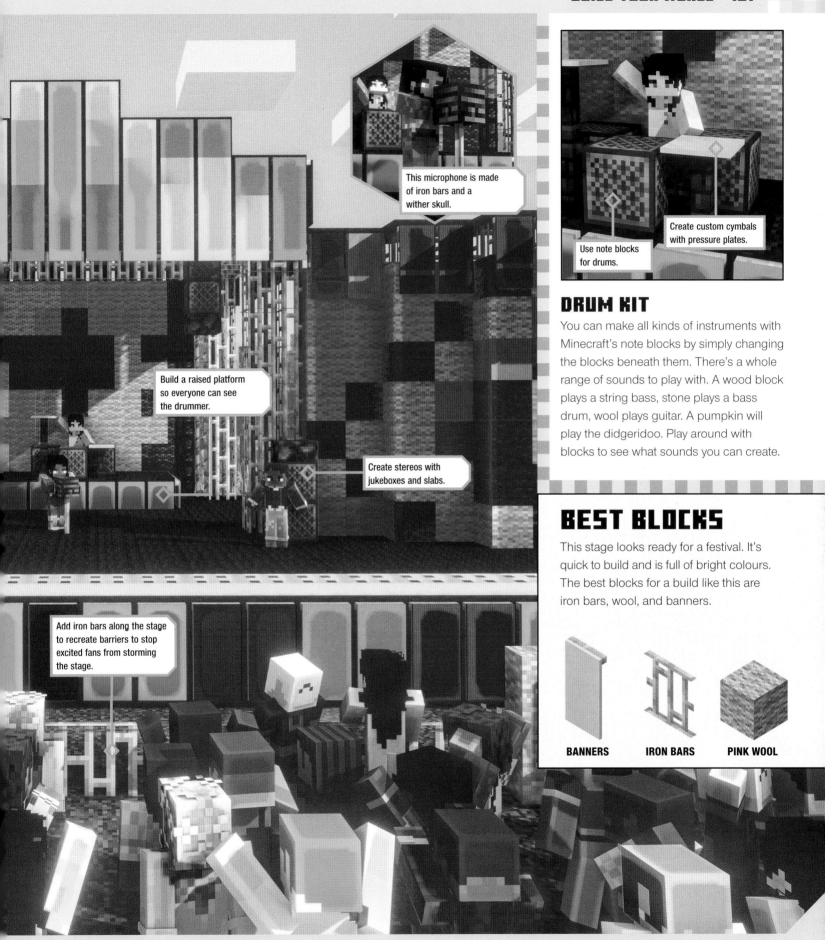

This microphone is made of iron bars and a wither skull.

Use note blocks for drums.

Create custom cymbals with pressure plates.

Build a raised platform so everyone can see the drummer.

Create stereos with jukeboxes and slabs.

Add iron bars along the stage to recreate barriers to stop excited fans from storming the stage.

DRUM KIT

You can make all kinds of instruments with Minecraft's note blocks by simply changing the blocks beneath them. There's a whole range of sounds to play with. A wood block plays a string bass, stone plays a bass drum, wool plays guitar. A pumpkin will play the didgeridoo. Play around with blocks to see what sounds you can create.

BEST BLOCKS

This stage looks ready for a festival. It's quick to build and is full of bright colours. The best blocks for a build like this are iron bars, wool, and banners.

BANNERS   **IRON BARS**   **PINK WOOL**

SHOPPING CENTRE

Shopping centres are fun places to visit – whether you want to go shopping or not. They are bustling with people, and they have lots of imaginative window displays and cool, modern architectural features, too. Build a Minecraft shopping centre that you can keep expanding and adding to. Get creative and design a grand exterior with unique shopfronts inside to wow passersby.

BUILDING BRIEF

Key features: Large building with multiple floors and a central atrium (a hall with glass roof)

Added extras: Villager shops with all 13 professions (see more on p160–161)

Don't forget to: Add lighting to keep hostile mobs out!

Create a domed ceiling made from light blue stained glass.

BUILD TIP

Each shop has its own goods for sale and a villager to attend to the shoppers. You can add lots of different villager shops to this shopping centre, each selling different wares based on their trade. Showcase each villager's wares on armour stands and item frames.

A tall, raised canopy made of deepslate tile walls and slabs marks the entrance.

Add glass walls to let in lots of natural light.

BEST BLOCKS

The walls of this shopping centre are made of smooth sandstone and white concrete, while the floors use stripped jungle wood. Add a wall of glass blocks to let players see the enticing shops inside.

STRIPPED JUNGLE WOOD

SMOOTH SANDSTONE

THE REAL DEAL

It is super snowy in Montreal, Canada, so the city's main shopping centre has been built underground. It's known as Underground City and stretches for about 33 km (about 20.5 miles). As well as more than 2,000 shops, there are 200 restaurants, ten metro stations, and several cinemas.

Fill large spaces with natural features such as living walls.

Build a set of stairs to lead shoppers to the underground car park.

BUILD HIGHLIGHTS

Shopping centres are usually busy places, so make sure to include big, open spaces in your Minecraft build for shoppers to walk around freely. However, large spaces can feel empty, so add small details, such as plants and colourful art, to bring the shopping centre to life.

CENTRAL ATRIUM

All the build's shops and facilities are arranged around a central atrium. Its glass roof adds lots of light and the walls are decorated in bright colours. The staircases and corridors help shoppers to navigate around the mall.

CALM ZONES

Shopping can be tiring, so you can provide quiet areas for shoppers to sit and rest. Use stair blocks to create benches and add quartz slab tables.

SHOPPING CENTRE: INTERIOR

A shopping centre offers so much more than a collection of stores. There are usually lots of different cafés and restaurants, plus cinemas and even play areas for younger kids. What will you include in your Minecraft shopping centre? You could add a gym, a petting zoo, or even an arcade!

Place stained glass panes in a zig-zag pattern for decoration.

PLAYER SHOP

Players often have lots of things they want to trade, so invite friends to open shops of their own. This shop owner is selling survival equipment like chests, beds, and crafting tables. They also have rare amethyst clusters for sale.

VILLAGER SHOP

Prepare shopfronts for your villagers. Bring villagers to the shops and give them appropriate job blocks. Villagers will trade items depending on their jobs. This villager is a weaponsmith and uses a grindstone job block.

Join each floor with polished andesite stairs and andesite walls.

RESTAURANT

Mangrove stair seats and piston tables make a cosy restaurant area. Add fun decorations, such as candles and dead corals. You could build long cafeteria-style tables instead.

BUILD TIP

There's space here for all the villagers to peddle their wares. Build shopfronts for each of the 13 different professions. When they're built, spawn or bring a villager with the appropriate job and give them the job block they need. They'll trade their goods for emeralds. A butcher uses a smoker, a cartographer uses a cartography table, a shepherd uses a loom, a weaponsmith uses a grindstone, and so on.

Add pizzazz to the shopping experience with some modern art. These hanging pieces are made with colourful blocks, buttons, and levers.

Create stall-sized shops and give each one its own theme. This shop has mob skulls and flowerpots for sale.

LOOK CLOSER

You will need to ensure your shopping centre stays well lit for the safety of your shoppers. Light up dark corners with quirky lighting such as lanterns, froglights, and End rods. It will also make the shopping centre feel warm and welcoming.

Mix and match the flooring blocks. The ground floor is mostly granite and stripped log tiling, but there's also light grey carpet in some areas.

FIREWORKS

Boom, crackle, pop! Fireworks have been popular for more than 2,000 years. Historians believe early fireworks were made from bamboo sticks filled with gunpowder. Firework shows are put on throughout the year to mark special occasions, such as Lunar New Year, Independence Day in the USA, Guy Fawkes Night in the UK, and many more. Mark your own special occasions in Minecraft with a colourful firework show. Or why not make every day a day to celebrate by crafting your own special permanent firework display? Here, permanent fireworks are mixed with exploding Minecraft fireworks for a spectacular display.

BUILDING BRIEF

Key features: Permanent stained glass fireworks, Minecraft firework explosions

Added extras: Special-effect fireworks

Don't forget to: Step back from the firework display to get the best view

BUILD TIP

These permanent fireworks are a fantastic display by day or night. For these fireworks to light up the night sky, try building the explosions out of glowstone or light blocks instead of stained glass. You can also add an invisible light source using a command.

Mix any of the 16 coloured glass blocks to create unique patterns for your permanent fireworks.

Create a creeper head-shaped firework by adding any mob head when crafting an exploding Minecraft firework.

THE REAL DEAL

Just like in Minecraft, real fireworks have special ingredients that determine the colour that bursts out. Yellow fireworks use sodium compounds while blue fireworks use copper ones. Lots of fireworks were needed for the world's biggest firework display, which was held in the Philippines in 2016. Over 810,000 fireworks were set off in a show that lasted for over an hour!

Make your permanent fireworks in small and giant sizes.

Add a gold nugget to your exploding Minecraft fireworks to create a star effect.

AN EXPLOSIVE DISPLAY

There are a whopping 29 quintillion combinations of available firework explosions in Minecraft. To begin crafting a firework rocket, you'll need to start with a firework star. Use gunpowder and your chosen dye to craft a firework star, then combine it with paper and gunpowder to create a firework rocket. You can also add special effects – try adding a fire charge, gold nugget, mob head, feather, diamond, or glowstone dust when crafting the firework star. If you add more firework stars to your firework rocket it will create a larger, wilder explosion.

FIREWORK DISPENSER

Create a firework dispenser using a dispenser, redstone repeater, redstone dust, redstone torch, and a lever. When you're ready, fill the dispenser with fireworks – then flip the lever to start the show.

BEST BLOCKS

The permanent fireworks are slightly see-through and colourful. They're made out of stained glass blocks. Build each firework in the colour of your choice or if you're up for a challenge, try merging several colours together.

PURPLE STAINED GLASS

BLUE STAINED GLASS

SWIMMING POOL

Every community needs a local swimming pool – and the facilities at this Minecraft pool are top-notch. There's even a café on site to keep parents busy so you can stay for just five more minutes. Design your own pool for swimming laps, taking a leap from the diving board, or for simply splashing around.

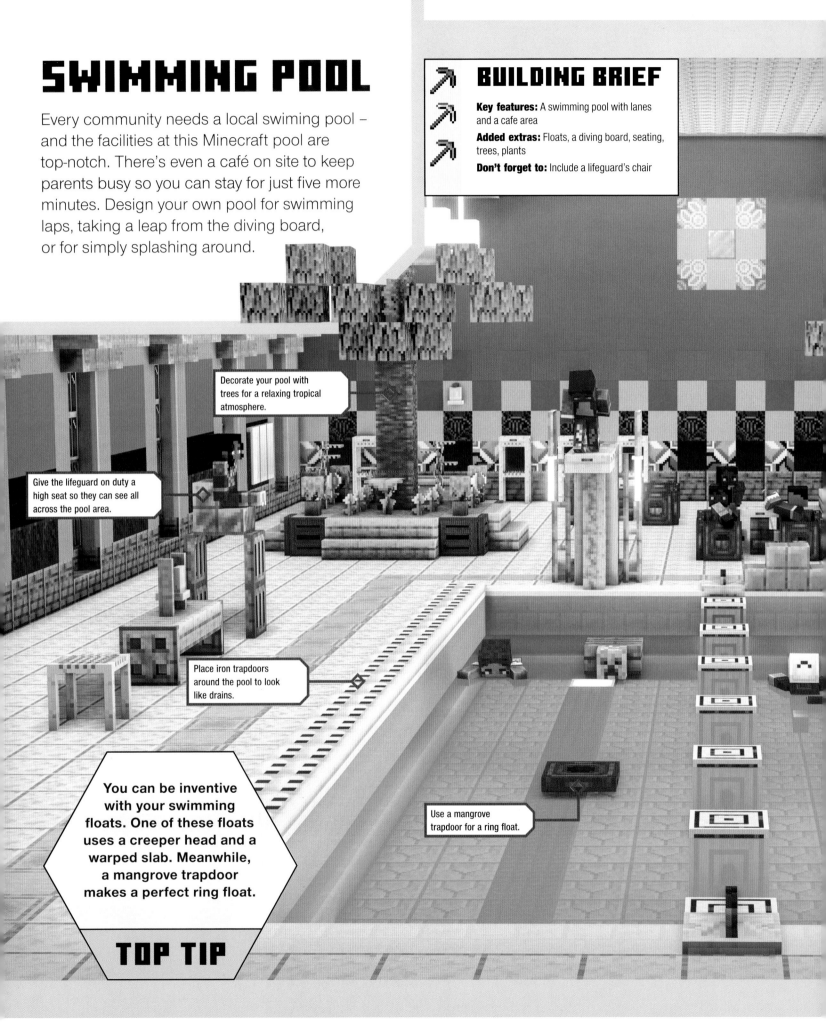

Decorate your pool with trees for a relaxing tropical atmosphere.

Give the lifeguard on duty a high seat so they can see all across the pool area.

Place iron trapdoors around the pool to look like drains.

Use a mangrove trapdoor for a ring float.

TOP TIP

You can be inventive with your swimming floats. One of these floats uses a creeper head and a warped slab. Meanwhile, a mangrove trapdoor makes a perfect ring float.

THE REAL DEAL

There are lots of unusual pools in the world to be inspired by. There's the Sky Pool in the UK, which has a glass bottom and looks like it is floating between two buildings. You'll even find guitar-shaped and heart-shaped pools in the USA. At the Marina Bay Sands hotel, Singapore, there is an infinity pool where swimmers can enjoy views from 57 storeys up.

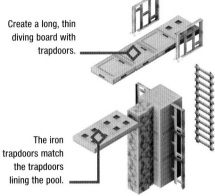

Create a long, thin diving board with trapdoors.

The iron trapdoors match the trapdoors lining the pool.

DIVING BOARD

In Minecraft, landing in water prevents fall damage. Unlike diving in the real world, you can jump from any height and land safely if you land in water. Build a diving platform to test it out. This board is four blocks high, but yours can be as tall as you like. No matter how high it is, you won't take fall damage if you land in the pool.

Take a rest from all the activity on loungers made from beds and birch trapdoors.

IN THE CAFÉ

Swimming is tiring work, so enjoy some milk and cake at the café to replenish your energy levels. The seating area uses cut waxed cut copper slabs and mangrove trapdoors for chairs and a deepslate tile wall with a birch trapdoor on top for a table.

Add lanes for lap swimmers using target blocks and chains.

BEST BLOCKS

Build an enticing-looking pool using polished diorite, which looks sparkling clean. Prismarine bricks and dark prismarine capture that classic blue pool look.

POLISHED DIORITE

PRISMARINE BRICKS

DARK PRISMARINE

CLIMBING WALL

Climbing walls are a fun activity for building strength and stamina, and they'll teach you to problem-solve and plan ahead at the same time, too. Climbing is a huge part of Minecraft, whether it's scaling mountains or clambering out of caves. Get some practice in with your own climbing wall. Using a mix of blocks will test your skills to the max because each block type has its own surface area. Once you can calculate the jump, it's a quick climb to the top.

LOOK CLOSER

In Survival mode, scaling any climbing wall brings the risk of fall damage so make your floor safe with slime blocks. They not only prevent all fall damage and make you bounce, but they can also be covered with bright carpets. Hay bales are another option, they will reduce fall damage by up to 80 percent.

Place scaffolding along the side for an easy way back down the wall.

Stepping on a big dripleaf will cause it to tilt and drop you. It will reset to its original position after a few seconds.

Make footholds from unusual blocks such as cocoa beans, trapdoors, and small amethyst buds.

Decorate the slime flooring by adding colourful carpet on top.

THE REAL DEAL

The world's tallest indoor climbing wall is in the New World City shopping mall in Shanghai, China. Measuring a mountainous 51.28 m (168 ft), it is around the same height as a 14-storey building.

Add wooden blocks to reach the beginning of the climbing course.

Use colourful banners to decorate the walls.

Add obstacles to your wall, such as buttons and tripwire hooks.

You'll need fast fingers to open and shut a trapdoor ladder in time to climb.

VINES AND LADDERS

You can climb and jump from ladders and vines, and creating a course with these two climbing blocks is pretty simple. However, that doesn't mean the course has to be easy to climb. Build some obstacles with the vines and ladders, and keep practising so you can get to the top of these tricky routes.

The big dripleaf will tip over after around one second.

SPEEDRUN

Build a dripleaf circuit to test your players' speed. First you will need to place grass on the ground to plant your big dripleaf, because you can't grow a big dripleaf on concrete. Then use bone meal to grow the plant in height. Dripleaf routes will have players rushing. If they stick around too long, the big dripleaf will tip and drop them!

BEST BLOCKS

The best blocks to use will depend on how challenging you want your wall to be. You can use traditional climbing blocks such as vines and ladders or include trapdoors, skulls, chains, and fences for a greater challenge.

VINES   **LADDER**

AQUARIUM

An aquarium can be a small-scale home for some cute fishy pets or a large-scale tank built to protect and study unusual marine creatures. Whatever the size or purpose of an aquarium, the tank will need to be sturdy enough not to crack from the pressure of the water inside. Use your imagination to recreate an aquarium in Minecraft. Think about what interesting and colourful habitats you can create for the creatures inside your tank, and how you can keep them happy and healthy.

BUILDING BRIEF

Key features: Glass tank, colourful coral, kelp

Added extras: Rocks, underwater features such as wooden structures

Don't forget to: Include a book with information about your fish

Coral blocks have five variants: tube, brain, bubble, fire, and horn.

Add bright purple amethyst clusters to decorate the aquarium.

This cross-section shows the glass blocks that recreate the thick, sturdy glass used in aquariums.

Mangrove roots can be placed underwater and will fill with water, becoming waterlogged.

Use fences to create interesting wooden structures for your aquarium creatures to play and hide in.

THE REAL DEAL

The largest aquarium in the world is Chimelong Ocean Kingdom in China. Its tanks contains almost 49 million litres (13 million gallons) of water – that's nearly as much as 20 Olympic-sized swimming pools! It has around 8 million visitors a year.

Add a book with information on all the wildlife living in the aquarium.

COLOURFUL CORAL

Real coral reefs are actually formed by tiny marine creatures and their skeletons. In Minecraft, coral blocks are available in five colours and are perfect for creating a colourful tank decoration. Coral needs to be next to water or a waterlogged block to survive, and it is often found alongside sea pickles. If coral is placed outside water it transforms into dead coral within about five seconds.

CREATING BUBBLES

Creating a bubble column in Minecraft is super simple. All you need is dirt, soul sand, kelp, and bone meal. Place a dirt block on the ground and add a piece of kelp. Use bone meal to grow kelp to the surface, then remove the kelp and replace the dirt block with a soul sand block. For a reverse bubble column, you can use a magma block instead of a dirt block.

BEST BLOCKS

The best block for a fish tank is glass, so players can see what's inside. Add seagrass, kelp, mangrove roots, and big dripleaves to make the aquarium a fun and colourful place to swim around in.

GLASS

SEAGRASS

FUNFAIR

Roll up, roll up! Come and buy a ticket for the Overworld's biggest Ferris wheel, if you dare. Packed with rides to make you scream with excitement (and sometimes terror), this funfair has fun for all the family. Try your luck at the throwing practice, have a go at driving the bumper boats, and take a deep breath before strapping in to the minecart roller coaster. Collect as many tokens as possible to win a prized golden carrot.

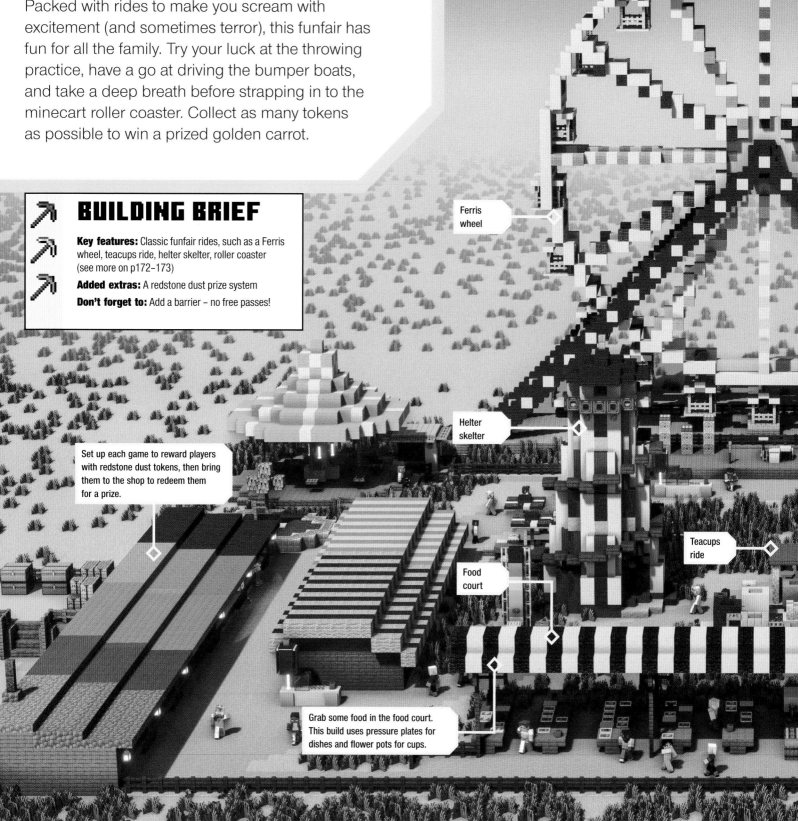

BUILDING BRIEF

Key features: Classic funfair rides, such as a Ferris wheel, teacups ride, helter skelter, roller coaster (see more on p172–173)

Added extras: A redstone dust prize system

Don't forget to: Add a barrier – no free passes!

Ferris wheel

Set up each game to reward players with redstone dust tokens, then bring them to the shop to redeem them for a prize.

Helter skelter

Teacups ride

Food court

Grab some food in the food court. This build uses pressure plates for dishes and flower pots for cups.

THE REAL DEAL

The tallest Ferris wheel in the world is the Ain Dubai (Dubai Eye), in the UAE. It's 250 m (820 ft) tall, which is the equivalent of a 58-storey building. It takes 38 minutes to complete a full rotation and can take a whopping 1,920 visitors at a time.

BUILD TIP

Create colourful patterns to make your fairground build stand out. You can start by simply alternating blocks to create checks and stripes, like on the food court and Ferris wheel. For more advanced and intricate designs, place frames with items in them, like the yellow details seen at the top of the swingboat structure.

BUILD HIGHLIGHTS

Invite friends to visit your funfair and create games for them to play. This funfair has more than a dozen Minecraft-working games you could recreate, such as bumper boats, roller coasters, a throwing game, and a target gallery!

BUMPER BOATS

This twist on a classic game uses boats instead of cars. Create an arena and use different wood types for different coloured boats. Then fill the floor with ice blocks. Place all the different boats in the arena and get ready to bump!

THROWING PRACTICE

Create a fun throwing activity to play with your friends, based on a basketball arcade game. Take turns to hit the target block with an arrow. This opens the trapdoor, revealing a hopper for you to throw an item into. Score!

Use minecarts and rails to create attractions such as roller coasters and haunted houses.

Swingboat

Roller coaster

Merry-go-round

Bumper boats

Decorate your arcade booth to make it look enticing.

BEST BLOCKS

You can use any type of blocks you like for this fairground build, because the focus is on colour. This build uses every colour of wool you can possibly get in Minecraft.

YELLOW WOOL

RED WOOL

FUNFAIR: FUNCTIONING ATTRACTIONS

Building a fairground gives you endless opportunities to be creative. There are lots of blocks you can use in Minecraft to create functioning attractions, such as this roller coaster ride and target gallery. Arcade games are a fantastic way to improve your redstone skills, too. Try building these games, and then have a go at making up your own thrilling games and rides.

POWERED RAILS

Powered rails automatically push the mine carts forwards. Place them near bumps in the roller coaster to help propel the minecarts over the top. Add redstone torches or levers to keep them active.

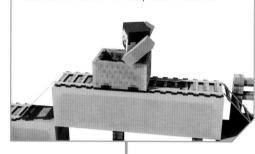

ROLLER COASTER

No fairground is complete without an epic roller coaster. This working Minecraft roller coaster uses rails and powered rails to send players racing along the tracks. What could be more fun than a fast, wild ride around a circuit in a minecart?

CHANGE IT!

If you don't want to use redstone, change the roller coaster into a steam train by using a minecart with a furnace. Place it on the rails, and have a stack of fuel ready to power the furnace and send the minecarts racing around the circuit.

Use concrete, mangrove slabs, and glass panes to build a small ticket booth.

Don't forget to add queuing lanes next to your attractions.

TARGET GALLERY

This is another classic fairground game that works really well in Minecraft. Players can aim bows at the target blocks to win prizes. Hit a target to light the redstone lamp and win a prize. Challenge yourself to shoot all the targets as fast as you can.

Hitting the target lights the redstone lamp.

Getting a bullseye will light a second redstone lamp!

Showcase the prizes you can win.

BULLSEYE!

The target gallery is made of target blocks and redstone lamps. When hit, a target block will send a redstone signal to the redstone lamps to light them up.

ARROWS

This dropper is full of arrows. You just need to press the button to release one. Do not use a dispenser instead; the arrows will shoot you!

Minecarts are pushed around in a loop by powered rails.

Start building your roller coaster with a concrete block outline. Then place your rails on blocks.

Use fences to elevate the track and transform your ride into a bumpy roller coaster.

COMMUNITY GARDEN

Community gardens or parks are wonderful places to surround yourself with nature, relax, play, and meet other people. This beautiful Minecraft urban garden has something for all ages. There's a fun playground for kids, walking routes, and even shared gardening spaces for all the local community. What will you include in your Minecraft garden?

Pumpkins grow in this vegetable patch. What will you choose to grow in yours?

Build beehives for bees to live in. Bees are helpful pollinators, moving pollen from flower to flower, and causing more plants to grow.

Packing lots of colour into your Minecraft garden is easy with wild flowers – they will grow anywhere where there is grass. Use bone meal on the grass blocks. You can also craft wild flowers, such as poppies, into dye. You can then add colourful blocks to your garden, like the slide's red blocks.

LOOK CLOSER

THE REAL DEAL

Green spaces are very important to real towns and cities. They combat some of the effects of pollution, improve air quality, and boost biodiversity (different types of animal and plant life). Studies show green spaces are beneficial to physical and mental health, and they strengthen ties to the community, too.

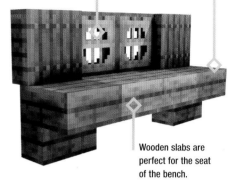

Create patterns on the backrest by using jungle wood trapdoors.

This bench uses spruce wood stairs for the ends of the bench and legs.

Wooden slabs are perfect for the seat of the bench.

Add oak wood, trapdoors, fences, and extra leaves to an existing tree to make it much bigger.

Create climbing equipment with a slide and a sliding pole.

Stone walkways connect every corner of the garden together.

TAKE A SEAT

Every park needs some benches – whether for sitting, reading, picnicking, or just daydreaming and watching the world go by. These benches use a simple design of stairs, slabs, and trapdoors. The choice of wood helps them blend in with the park's leafy background.

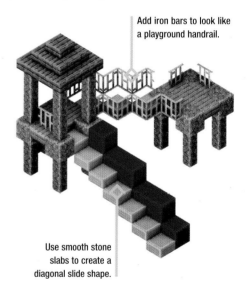

Add iron bars to look like a playground handrail.

Use smooth stone slabs to create a diagonal slide shape.

PLAYGROUND FUN

You can include lots of cool features in your playground. This build has a slide, a climbing platform, and a sliding pole. You could add a climbing wall, monkey bars, a roundabout, or a seesaw. The floor can be part of the fun too, with a hopscotch or checkerboard design, or sand, like this one. Think about the best parks you've ever played in and recreate them in Minecraft.

BEST BLOCKS

Finding a flower forest biome will set you on track to gather all the blocks you need. Grass, stone, and leaves are everywhere. If you find some skeletons, defeat them for their bones to make bone meal.

GRASS

STONE

LEAVES

GREEN HOME

Designing a home in Minecraft is a really fun way to think about practical ways to be green. Being green, or living sustainably, means thinking about how we live and the things we use so that we can help to protect our planet and its natural resources. Reusing or repurposing things rather than throwing them away is a good start. Build your Minecraft home using sustainable and renewable materials. Choose blocks that won't run out, or that you can easily grow or make more of.

Stone can be crafted by smelting cobblestone in a furnace. Power the furnace with dried kelp blocks. They burn for longer than coal, and are renewable.

Add a rain chain. In the real world, these collect water, which trickles down to plants.

Wood is the perfect sustainable block choice for your green home. There are many types of wood and hyphae you can choose from. Before starting your build, plant a forest of all the wood types you want to use to keep your inventory full.

TOP TIP

Growing your own food is very sustainable. Keep composters handy to recycle excess food by using it as compost for the soil.

THE REAL DEAL

About 20 per cent of global energy comes from renewable energy supplies, such as solar power, wind power, and hydropower (water power). Iceland produces all of its energy from its renewable sources. It uses hydropower and geothermal energy (natural heat within Earth, which is used to generate electricity).

UNDERGROUND FRIDGE

Did you know that normal fridges consume lots of energy? Create a natural fridge in Minecraft for fun instead. In real life, temperatures are cooler underground, so make an eco-fridge like this one by burying the appliance below ground. This fridge is an underground iron block box with chests for storing your food.

Maximize green space with a roof garden. Use moss or grass blocks with bone meal to grow plants.

Redstone lamps are connected to daylight detectors to provide renewable energy.

WIND POWER

Wind turbines have harnessed the natural power of the wind for centuries. Reimagine this sustainable energy source in Minecraft with your own wind-turbine-shaped builds. Use birch fences, birch planks with a polished blackstone button, and four birch trapdoors as wings. Place them around your home – and even on the roof.

BEST BLOCKS

Focus on renewable materials that you can create in-game, such as cobblestone and grass. Enchant a tool with Silk Touch so you can also reuse and recycle non-renewable blocks such as glass.

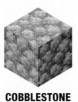

COBBLESTONE

GRASS

GLASS

FUTURISTIC CITY

What will our cities look like in the future? With populations increasing, cities need to provide homes, power, and jobs for billions of people. All around the world, people are thinking about how cities can be made better for the environment and their residents. Test out your clever city planning ideas in Minecraft. How will the buildings look and what will they be made from? Where will you add green spaces? What environmentally friendly transportation could you add? There's a lot to think about!

BUILDING BRIEF

Key features: Lots of tall buildings of different shapes and styles, plenty of parks and green spaces

Added extras: A vertical farm, tramways (see more on p180), solar panels

Don't forget to: Research clever ideas for sustainable cities

Make your city actually green with living walls made of leaves.

Add a windmill to your build. In the real world, wind turbines use natural winds to generate electricity. They are a great addition to any city.

> You can start small and expand later. This futuristic city is a major building project, so you won't be able to finish it in one session. Start by planning the hub of a small city and then keep adding to and improving it.
>
> **TOP TIP**

Build raised walkways full of lush vegetation.

BEST BLOCKS

What's the best block of the future? That's for you to decide. This build features lots of fun green blocks to tie in with the green theme, like leaves, oxidized cut copper slabs, and even melons.

OXIDIZED CUT COPPER SLABS

MELON

THE REAL DEAL

As the world population nears 8 billion, it puts pressure on Earth's natural resources. Living sustainably means living in a way that could carry on for a long time without causing more damage to the planet. Using renewable energy that won't run out or create pollution, such as solar and wind power, is one way to do this.

BUILD HIGHLIGHTS

Take a look at where you live or places you have visited, and think about what works well and what you might change. From the shapes of buildings to the layouts of roads, decide what will be important for a city of the future.

Build upwards. Maximize the land space by adding extra levels to your buildings.

Daylight detectors are powered by light. They activate the redstone when the light level is high enough.

Add rooftop gardens to apartment blocks.

Create large, open spaces for players to socialize and relax.

GRID DESIGN

The simplest way to design a city is as a grid. Straight roads are easier to navigate, and using a grid design also saves blocks when building. A grid layout won't prevent you from adding your individual style to your buildings. Just use lots of colour and patterns.

CLOSE TO NATURE

Plan lots of parks and nature reserves so trees, plants, and animals can thrive in your city, too. Green spaces help to keep the air clean and are important for people's physical and mental health.

FUTURISTIC CITY: MODERN DESIGNS

As our technology develops, the way we build and design our cities changes, too. Today, many cities are already showcasing unique architecture and transport systems. This Minecraft build features an electric tram and round high-rises. How will your futuristic city look? Remember, it doesn't have to look anything like the cities we have today.

BUILD TIP

Let your imagination take over. No one knows what cities will look like in the future, so you can design your city however you like. Some parts may not work in Minecraft – yet. New blocks are added to Minecraft every year to inspire ideas and to be added to your builds.

ELECTRIC TRAM

Trams were first invented around 150 years ago, and they are still a great way of beating traffic jams in big cities today. They run on electricity, which can be generated from renewable sources such as sun and wind. This simple, box-shaped tram doesn't run in Minecraft, but shows how your futuristic city might work.

Real trams are connected to power lines overhead. These lines are recreated on this build with chains and levers.

In the real world, these carriages are made with lightweight materials. They use less energy to run, making them better for the environment.

Use as many glass blocks as possible to give passengers the best view.

Add seats inside the tram for passengers' comfort.

Use copper blocks to make the front headlights and oxidized copper for the back.

Create tracks with ridges for tram wheels. This build uses andesite walls and stairs, chiselled stone bricks, and polished diorite.

BUILDING DESIGN

Round buildings are more energy-efficient than square buildings. This is because they use fewer resources to build, make better use of heating, and capture more natural light. So ditch the corners and try building some rounded high-rise buildings in Minecraft.

SOLAR ENERGY

The roofs of tall buildings are ideal for solar panels. This Minecraft solar panel is made from polished blackstone and light weighted pressure plates, and sits on top of a quartz stairs structure.

Ochre froglights

Lightning rods have soul torches on top.

Both sides have living walls made using some variants of plant leaves.

Choose your favourite blocks and use them to style the build. This high-rise uses lots of oxidised copper and concrete.

Each floor is 7 blocks tall from floor to ceiling.

Style the windows with slabs. These oxidized cut copper slabs allow light in without blocking the view.

ROUND SHAPE

To build this structure, create a round base that is 24 blocks in diameter (from one point to another). When you have the round shape, you can build the walls. Keep adding blocks to the walls until the building is as tall as you'd like.

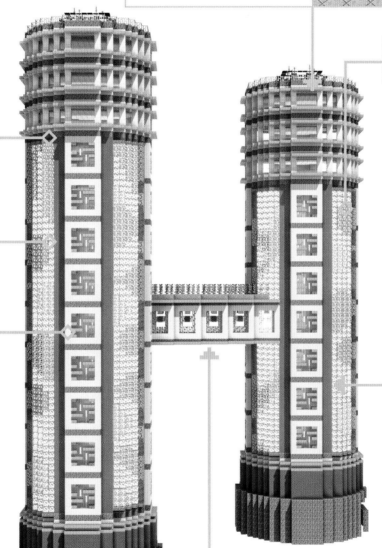

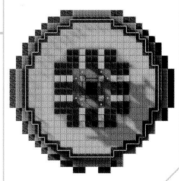

BRIDGES

High-rise buildings are sometimes joined by bridges to make travelling between them easier. This bridge also boasts a spectacular view over the city. Don't forget to add iron bars for safety.

This high-rise is 96 blocks tall from the ground to the top of the redstone torches.

CHANGE IT!

High-rises in Minecraft maximize the use of space above your head, but you can change this build to fit your needs. Does it need to be even taller or wider? Can you install a bubble lift (see p113 for more details) to reach the top floor?

MODERN FARM

When we learned to farm, about 12,000 years ago, it changed the way humans live. Being able to grow our own food allowed us to settle in one place and build towns. As the global population has increased, so has the demand for food. It's a good thing modern farmers have found clever ways to grow more food in smaller spaces, such as vertical farms. Can you take your Minecraft farm to the next level?

BUILDING BRIEF

Key features: Repeatable farming floors, a storage barn

Added extras: Potted flowers, composter

Don't forget to: Place plenty of water and light sources

Slate-like blackstone slabs and blocks help the farm blend into an urban environment.

This farm has five tiers of farmland. That's an excellent use of space.

THE REAL DEAL

Organic farming is the most green method of food production. However, it yields fewer crops than farming using chemicals. Increasing available farmland with vertical farms will allow us to produce food without destroying wild habitats. Plant waste can also be turned into biofuels that will meet some of our energy demands. They are more environmentally friendly than fossil fuels, like coal and oil, because crops absorb carbon from the atmosphere as they grow.

BUILD HIGHLIGHTS

When land space is limited, just build upwards. In a vertical farm, different crops can be grown on each floor. You'll need an irrigation system for all those crops, too.

Dark oak signs blend in with dark oak trapdoors to hide the farmland blocks.

Add a slab floor to make the most out of the limited space.

VERTICAL FARM

In this build, the farmland is wide enough to be harvested by hand while the floors are low enough to fit as many stories as possible into a small space. Each floor is three blocks tall and features the essentials – crops, water, and light sources.

IRRIGATION

Crops need water to grow, so every farm needs a good irrigation system (water supply). The most effective layout for your farm is one water source with farmland extending four blocks in every direction around it.

This barn for storing harvested food uses brick, terracotta, and concrete.

Add stripped oak logs and andesite walls to create a unique look.

Don't let food go to waste. Place composters, which you can use to craft bone meal from your excess crops.

Build potted plants using birch trapdoors, dirt, and your favourite flowers.

TOP TIP

Real crops need sunlight to grow but in Minecraft, any kind of light will work. Include light sources like lanterns in your build so that your crops can grow through the day and night.

WATER

DIRT

BEST BLOCKS

Building a Minecraft farm requires two essential blocks – dirt and water – and one vital tool – a hoe. You can grow a variety of crops, from vegetables such as carrots, to grains including wheat, and even some fruit like melons.

WINTER SPORTS RESORT

Snow-covered mountains are ideal for winter sports like skiing, snowboarding, and tobogganing. The steeper the slope, the faster you can go. Find a tall, snowy mountain in Minecraft and keep adding blocks to make it as high as you can. For a wild ride, turn a boat into a toboggan and slide down the snowy slopes. Think about what else you might build to make your Minecraft winter resort the coolest place around.

BUILDING BRIEF

Key features: Steep slides designed for maximum tobogganing speed

Added extras: Wooden chalets, ski lift

Don't forget to: Add street lanterns to melt snow and ice and keep the paths clear

LOOK CLOSER

Make your snowy piste fit for racing. Minecraft boats can move on any surface, but they go faster on ice than on any other. Use a mix of snow, ice, and diorite to create different obstacles for your racers and to alter the speed of the course. Ready, set, go!

Add paths, including markers and obstacles, for the winter sports.

Snow collects on the ground in up to eight layers.

Give every home a shovel for digging out after a snow fall.

Place lanterns along the footpaths to melt the snow and ice here. This works in Minecraft and in the real world!

THE REAL DEAL

Riding a toboggan is all about the speed you need to get to the bottom of the hill! There are a variety of forms of tobogganing to try, such as luge, bobsleigh, and skeleton. The world record for the fastest downhill toboggan was set by Guy Martin in Andorra. He reached a speedy 134.37 km/h (83.49 mph) in 2014.

If you build high enough in a snowy biome, it causes snow to collect naturally.

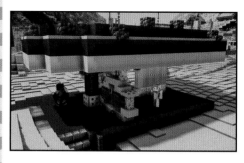

SKI LIFT

A real-life ski lift travels up a mountain on a cable circuit, carrying thrill-seekers to the peak. In this Minecraft version, skiiers can queue at a building for their turn. The booth has a redstone gate that limits the number of players at a time to recreate waiting for a lift. The gate opens and closes every 30 seconds.

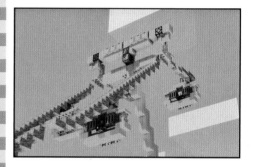

REACHING THE TOP

Flickering redstone lamps along the ski lift replicate the signal when the ski lift is ready for passengers. Place three redstone repeaters inside the standing posts to set the speed of the flickering light.

SKI CHALET

Build simple wooden chalets for your visitors to relax in after a busy day on the slopes. You could kit out the interiors with a cauldron boiling stew over a campfire, cosy carpets, and comfortable chairs.

BEST BLOCKS

If you build in the right biome, snow will generate naturally, but to create this resort you will still need to build the wooden chalets. Use lots of spruce planks, trapdoors, and doors, plus barrels for extra detailing.

SPRUCE PLANKS

BARRELS

FOOTBALL STADIUM

Do you wish your Minecraft world had a football tournament? Recreate your own cup final in a spectacular open-air stadium. You can make your stadium as big or small as you like – just make sure there is capacity to seat plenty of football fans of both teams. Include some concession stands for hungry spectators, too. Build your favourite team's stadium and recreate them winning the big game by handing out the winners' trophy. Put on your team's colours and get ready to cheer them on in Minecraft!

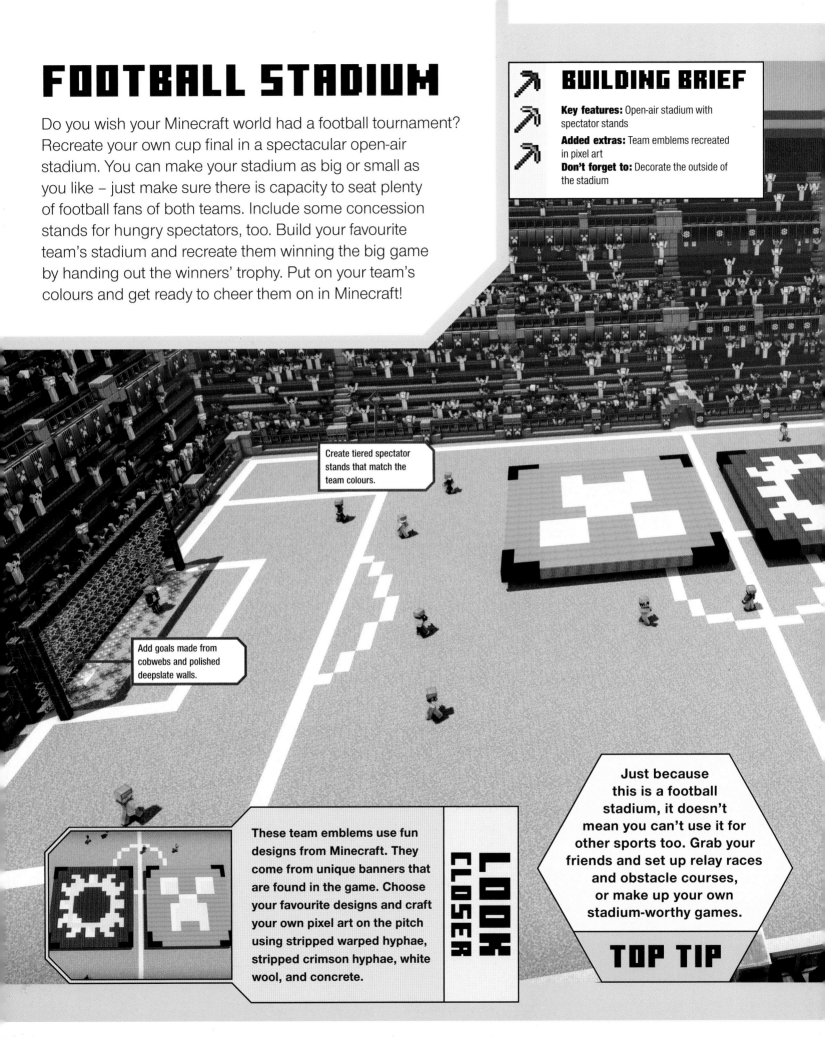

Create tiered spectator stands that match the team colours.

Add goals made from cobwebs and polished deepslate walls.

These team emblems use fun designs from Minecraft. They come from unique banners that are found in the game. Choose your favourite designs and craft your own pixel art on the pitch using stripped warped hyphae, stripped crimson hyphae, white wool, and concrete.

LOOK CLOSER

Just because this is a football stadium, it doesn't mean you can't use it for other sports too. Grab your friends and set up relay races and obstacle courses, or make up your own stadium-worthy games.

TOP TIP

THE REAL DEAL

Football is the most popular sport in the world, enjoyed by billions of people. The origins of the game can be found in ancient ball games played in every corner of the globe. But the very first dedicated football club, Sheffield FC, was established in 1857 in the UK. The professional game spread to every continent in just over a century.

Line the spectator stands with decorative banners.

Build stone step aisles between rows of seating.

Use white concrete powder to clearly mark the pitch lines.

There are no footballs in Minecraft, so use a mob skull for display instead.

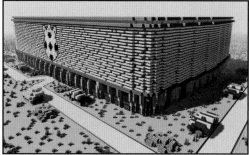

DECORATION

The huge football symbol in pixel art above the entrance leaves no doubt about what this building is for. Create the pixel art using coal, concrete, and wool blocks. Think about what else you could add to the outside of your stadium. Research famous football stadiums and see if you can recreate any of their colourful or distinctive features.

CONCESSION STANDS

Attending a live game is about more than just the football. It's an experience. Complete your stadium with some pop-up concession stands where fans can get team banners, drinks, and food. Place frames on the stand walls to advertise your wares and add oak stairs for tables. Banners make colourful decorations for the fronts of the stands.

BEST BLOCKS

This huge football stadium uses lots of different blocks. It needs grass for the pitch, stone for the walls, crimson and warped stairs for the seating, and cobwebs for the goal netting.

CRIMSON STAIRS

WARPED STAIRS

COBWEB

BOTANICAL GARDENS

In Minecraft and in the real world, different plants thrive under different conditions. Crops like wheat and beetroot need good irrigation (a water supply), but cactuses love to grow in gritty sand, and some plants thrive underwater. In a botanical garden, experts make sure that every plant has the conditions it needs, and they study the plants' development. Think about what you want to grow in your Minecraft botanical garden, and decide whether the garden will be open to visitors or just for you to enjoy.

BUILDING BRIEF

Key features: A greenhouse with a tall, domed glass ceiling to let in light

Added extras: A farmer villager to ensure the garden is well looked after

Don't forget to: Add lots of bee pollinators to keep your greenhouse buzzing with life

In Minecraft, a frog's colour depends on the biome it grows from a tadpole in. Frogs are orange in temperate biomes.

Place a flowering azalea into a plant pot so that you can move it around the greenhouse to the sunniest spot.

Add mossy cobblestones to the botanical garden's floor for texture.

Craft a path by using a shovel on grass blocks.

BEST BLOCKS

Glass block walls are the obvious choices for a botanical garden's greenhouse. Oxidized cut copper blocks are also a great addition to give the greenhouse a weathered appearance.

OXIDIZED CUT COPPER

GLASS BLOCK

THE REAL DEAL

The largest botanical garden in the world is Kew Gardens in the UK. The gardens are home to more than 27,000 plant species and are famous for the botanical research done there. It is estimated that one-third of all known plants have been preserved in botanical gardens around the world.

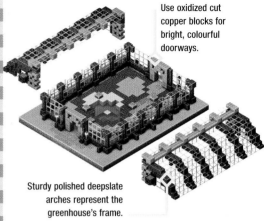

Use oxidized cut copper blocks for bright, colourful doorways.

Sturdy polished deepslate arches represent the greenhouse's frame.

Like real bees, Minecraft bees carry pollen. By pollinating plants, they accelerate the plant's growth.

Use bone meal on grass blocks to spawn lush green vegetation.

GREENHOUSE DESIGN

Botanical gardens often have greenhouses to create suitable habitats for plants that thrive in warmer or tropical conditions. This Minecraft greenhouse is made of glass blocks, which let in plenty of sunlight to keep the flowers growing. The build uses oxidized copper, polished deepslate, and glass to create the classic arched shape. You can build several greenhouses or one huge structure.

IRRIGATION IDEAS

All real-life plants need water to thrive, but some need more than others. In Minecraft, simply use a water bucket to place water and build a pond near your thirstiest blooms. It will hydrate up to four blocks in each direction. For plants that are further away, you can use your water bucket to create a stream.

TOP TIP

While grass is ideal for most plants, some plants like to live in other blocks. Place soul sand for growing Nether wart, sand for cactuses, and water for corals. You can even grow mushrooms on a podzol block.

THEATRE

Bring your performing and playwriting talents to the world of Minecraft with your very own Minecraft theatre. Get to work building a theatre and then write a play about a Minecraft adventure. You can ask your friends to become actors in your play, and when you're finished rehearsing, invite players to enjoy the show. With special seating and a big theatre stage, there's no better place to share your love of Minecraft.

BUILDING BRIEF

Key features: Stage, tiered rows of seating

Added extras: Redstone lamp engineering to turn the lights on and off

Don't forget to: Place banners around the Overworld to advertise your theatre

THE REAL DEAL

The first known theatre was built in Greece more than 2,500 years ago. The first plays were performed with just one lead actor (called a protagonist) and a chorus of people to help them tell the story.

On the upper level, use walls or glass panes to ensure safety without blocking anyone's view.

Add classic theatrical glamour with flooring made from red wool.

The flooring under the seats is polished blackstone. This durable material won't be ruined by spilt drinks and snack crumbs.

Use low-level lighting, such as these End rods beneath the stairs, to avoid complete darkness.

BEST BLOCKS

At a theatre, everyone needs to be able to see the stage. This model features tiered rows that are made from mangrove trapdoors and stripped mangrove logs.

MANGROVE TRAPDOOR

STRIPPED MANGROVE LOG

BUILD TIP

Take a moment to add some redstone engineering to your ceiling. These redstone lamps are connected with redstone dust to the lever. Flick the lever to turn the lights above the stage on when the show begins.

Create a stage to suit your show. This play is set in a modern town with a stone brick ground.

TIERED SEATING

Install cosy, 12-block-long, 2-block-wide rows of seats for your audience. First, place some black wool and blackstone on the floor for mood-setting. Then create the seating row with mangrove variants: mangrove logs, trapdoors, and stripped logs. Finish the rows off with crimson trapdoors on both ends, and hang colourful banners behind each seat.

ON STAGE

Shh! The show is starting. This theatre is a one-set wonder. The stage features a stone brick city courtyard with unique cars, shopfronts, and a podium for the narrator to start the story. You can build your own set for your show and find some actors to play each role. Will it be a city like this one, or perhaps a recreation of the End dimension to tell the tale of your defeat of the Ender Dragon? Build the stage using blocks from wherever your adventure takes place.

MEET THE BUILDERS

It takes creativity, passion, and countless hours of hard work to create the extraordinary builds featured in this book. Want to know how the builders do it and what inspires them? Find out below!

CYANA

USERNAME
CEa_TIde

LOCATION
The Netherlands

HAS PLAYED MINECRAFT FOR
10 long, fun years

What are your favourite things to build in Minecraft?
My favourites are organic builds (builds that are realistic and inspired by nature) and, more generally, asymmetric builds (builds that are not symmetrical). I also like to animate my builds, to make it look as if they're really moving and bustling with life.

What inspires you?
My mind is constantly searching for inspiration! It can be a situation in real life, pictures I come across online, or builds other people have made. I have a collection of these inspirations so I can look at them at any point.

What was the most challenging build for this book?
The Acropolis (p44–47) – it was challenging to make it as accurate as possible to how it would have been at the time.

What are your favourite things you've ever built in Minecraft?
One of my absolute favourite builds is a scene I made for the Lunar New Year, Year of the Tiger! It features a tiger walking through a Chinese gate on a street decorated with many lanterns. All the structures are based on real buildings in China, so I had lots of fun looking at references for those.

Statue of Athena from the Acropolis of Athens (p44–45)

ERIK LÖF

USERNAME
Kebabegott

LOCATION
Sweden

HAS PLAYED MINECRAFT FOR
Around 10–11 years

What are your favourite things to build in Minecraft?
I mostly like to build old stuff and realistic stuff.

What was your favourite thing to build for this book?
Al-Khazneh (The Treasury) in Petra (p52–53) is my favourite.

What's your top tip for beginners?
Don't be afraid to make mistakes and try out multiple styles. Don't stress about not being able to make something great the first time. You can always try again!

What's your favourite block or item?
I enjoy building with sandstone and mud.

Are there any blocks you like to use in unexpected ways?
Yes – one example is buttons. I find them perfect for adding small details, like adding texture on walls. I also like to use fence gates as decorative elements. They make excellent capitals on pillars or columns, adding a touch of elegance!

Al-Khazneh (The Treasury), Petra, Jordan (p52–53)

FROST_BEER

USERNAME
Frost_Beer

LOCATION
The Netherlands

**HAS PLAYED
MINECRAFT FOR**
11–12 years

What are your favourite things to build in Minecraft?
I love to recreate buildings and cities from real life – it's like building your own vacation! Every time you want to visit a certain country you can open Minecraft and experience it.

What inspires you?
I get most of my inspiration from history. I can't think of anything more interesting than studying how people built their structures and the thought that was put into every small detail.

What was your favourite thing to build for this book?
Either the Palaeontology Dig Site (p58–59) or Neuschwanstein Castle

(p30–31). Both turned out really accurate to the real structures.

What's your favourite block or item?
The brown mushroom block! Did you know that it secretly has two textures? When you place another brown mushroom block next to it and break it, you'll be left with a yellowish block with brown spots.

Are there any blocks you like to use in unexpected ways?
Yes, a brown candle on a green glass pane – if you then place these in the water it will look like a reed.

Neuschwanstein Castle, Germany
(p30–31)

GUILLAUME DUBOCAGE

USERNAME
MinecraftRepro

LOCATION
Czechia (Czech Republic), but originally from France

**HAS PLAYED
MINECRAFT FOR**
12 years

What are your favourite things to build in Minecraft?
Reproductions of real monuments and landmarks as well as large-scale aeroplanes.

What inspires you?
I'm inspired by the challenge of making builds as realistic as possible while respecting the scale constraints and sticking to vanilla Minecraft (Minecraft without user modifications).

What are your favourite things you've ever built in Minecraft?
The landmarks Mont Saint Michel (in France) and Prague's Castle, as well as a 10:1 scale reproduction of my favourite aircraft, the Mirage 2000C.

What's your top tip for beginners?
Plan ahead and use references. Use tools outside Minecraft to help with your builds. For example, you can convert blueprints to use in Minecraft so that you don't have to rely on guesswork for detailed builds.

What's your favourite block or item?
I like using stripped birch wood.

Are there any blocks you like to use in unexpected ways?
I use scaffolding for windows and banners for all sorts of details.

Château de Chenonceau, France
(p138–139)

HUGO

USERNAME
MYodaa

LOCATION
France

**HAS PLAYED
MINECRAFT FOR**
11 years

What are your favourite things to build in Minecraft?
My favourite things to build are large-scale structures such as realistic ships, as well as massive houses with intricate designs. I also enjoy building to-scale recreations of real-world buildings, such as the Eiffel Tower and other famous landmarks.

What inspires you?
I study different architectural styles and try to incorporate elements from them into my builds. I also draw inspiration from historical buildings and landmarks from around the world.

What's your top tip for beginners?
Start small and experiment with different building techniques, then gradually work your way up to more complex builds. Most importantly, have fun and patience!

What's your favourite block or item?
I like all of them! There is always a way to use blocks and items in unexpected ways.

Eiffel Tower, France (p56–57)

JAKOB GRAFE

USERNAME
RobJW

LOCATION
Germany

**HAS PLAYED
MINECRAFT FOR**
More than 10 years

What are your favourite things to build in Minecraft?
Giant explorable landscapes, medieval houses, and dwarven underground structures.

What inspires you?
I'm inspired by fantasy books and films, such as *The Lord of the Rings* and *Dune*, as well as digital art, and, of course, real architecture and places.

What are your favourite things you've ever built in Minecraft?
My favourite thing I've built is a giant medieval city that I worked on with my friends. Closely followed by a large spaceship and the Lacoste DLC (downloadable content) map

to celebrate the Lacoste x Minecraft apparel collection.

What's your top tip for beginners?
Don't be afraid to experiment with different ways of building, take your time, and, best of all, find a building buddy you can have fun with.

What's your favourite block or item?
My favourite block is the barrel and my favourite item is a glow item frame.

Are there any blocks you like to use in unexpected ways?
I love using sea pickles as salt and pepper shakers on tables.

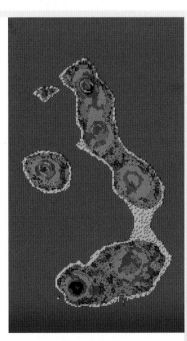

Galápagos Islands, Ecuador
(p94–95)

JÉRÉMIE TRIPLET

USERNAME
iTriplet

LOCATION
France

HAS PLAYED MINECRAFT FOR
6 years

What are your favourite things to build in Minecraft?
My favorite thing to do in Minecraft is building, but I also like playing Survival mode with the amazing community.

What was your favourite thing to build for this book?
My favorite build is the Futuristic City (p178–181). I want to inspire a new generation to be the architects of tomorrow.

What are your favourite things you've ever built in Minecraft?
I liked working on the Theatre build (p190–191) with CEa_Tlde. It was so much fun!

What's your top tip for beginners?
Try everything possible, be creative, and don't be afraid to do things differently.

What's your favourite block or item?
My favourite block is dark prismarine.

Theatre (p190–191)

JONATHIZE

USERNAME
Jonathize

LOCATION
Canada

HAS PLAYED MINECRAFT FOR
5 years

What are your favourite things to build in Minecraft?
I most like to build medieval structures and organic creatures.

What inspires you?
I'm inspired by testing my own creative limits.

What was your favourite thing to build for this book?
The Grand Bazaar of Istanbul (p136–137).

What's your top tip for beginners?
Learn how to use a large variety of blocks and then learn how they can work together. You can then apply this to bigger structures and builds.

What's your favourite block or item?
I like to use andesite blocks and spruce wood blocks.

Are there any blocks you like to use in unexpected ways?
Flowers in pots make great eyes for small organic creatures.

Lanterns from the Grand Bazaar, Istanbul (p136–137)

RUBEN SIX

USERNAME
mokie852

LOCATION
Belgium

HAS PLAYED MINECRAFT FOR
About 10 years

What are your favourite things to build in Minecraft?
I enjoy building creatures – sometimes humans.

What inspires you?
I'm mostly inspired by artwork created by other talented people and, of course, sci-fi movies.

What was your favourite thing to build for this book?
Definitely Angkor Wat (p54–55). I always wanted to recreate it but never took the time to do it.

What was your most challenging build for this book?
Surprisingly, it was the Plitvice Lakes (p100–101).

What are your favourite things you've ever built in Minecraft?
A realistic Warden and a Mosasaurus (an extinct marine reptile)!

What's your top tip for beginners?
References, references, references! Only by using detailed references as a guide will you see a lot of improvement in your builds.

What's your favourite block or item?
Warped roots – they have a very cool colour and can be used as hair for certain creatures.

Angkor Wat, Cambodia (p54–55)

SANDER POELMANS

USERNAME
Craftgig

LOCATION
Belgium

HAS PLAYED MINECRAFT FOR
More than 10 years (since the Pocket Edition came out)

What are your favourite things to build in Minecraft?
I like to build structures, terrain, and spaceships.

What was your favourite thing to build for this book?
The Rocket Launch Site (p122–125).

What was your most challenging build for this book?
The Rocket Launch Site, because making it simple enough to show in the book while still keeping in enough detail was a challenge.

What are your favourite things you've ever built in Minecraft?
Probably one of my large spaceships (more than 1,300 blocks long).

What's your top tip for beginners?
Don't be afraid to make mistakes! Try out as many different building styles as you can. By experimenting with styles you will learn a lot of new techniques that you can use in future builds.

What's your favourite block or item?
I have two – the terracotta blocks for adding colour to builds and the stripped woods for making buildings.

Are there any blocks you like to use in unexpected ways?
I use signs to add corner stones to buildings.

Rocket Launch Site (p122–123)

SONJA FIREHART

USERNAME
firehart

LOCATION
The Netherlands

**HAS PLAYED
MINECRAFT FOR**
Around 10 years

What was your favourite thing to build for this for this book?
Tropical Rainforest (p70–73)!

What was your most challenging build for this book?
The rainforest for sure. It required both my strongest and weakest building skills, so it was truly a challenge to make. I am loving it so much. I never had so much fun building structures!

What inspires you?
I'm inspired by nature, fantasy games, the Middle Ages, and lots of movies and TV shows such as *The Hobbit* and *Game of Thrones*.

What are your favourite things you've ever built in Minecraft?
Floating islands, huge medieval city islands, and grand fantasy castles surrounded by endless forests.

What's your top tip for beginners?
Try not to get discouraged. Building is a journey of practice and patience, and the more experience you have the easier it gets. Don't like your current build? Look at what you do like and what you don't like about it. Keep the "likes" and improve the "don'ts". Ask for feedback and look at other people's creations for inspiration. Always remember that building is supposed to be fun! It's not a race.

What's your favourite block or item?
I just love the elytra, I can't stop flying.

Tropical Rainforest (p70–73)

CHRISTIAN GLÜCKLICH

USERNAME
Cookiie

LOCATION
Germany

**HAS PLAYED
MINECRAFT FOR**
13 years

What are your favourite things to build in Minecraft?
I love building things with vibrant colours and interesting material combinations, but usually end up building something silly-looking instead. It's all about having fun!

What was your favourite thing to build for this book?
As the project build manager, I had the privilege of watching the amazingly talented builders create what you've seen on the pages of this book. I placed a few blocks here and there, but my favourite thing to build for this book was an amazing team!

What are your favourite things you've ever built in Minecraft?
My most favourite build, as of today, is a snail with big googly eyes staring at a rainbow.

What's your top tip for beginners?
Think outside the box, never give up, and have fun. Who cares if something looks silly if you had a lot of fun creating it?

Are there any blocks you like to use in unexpected ways?
You can make great solar panels with daylight sensors!

The building team

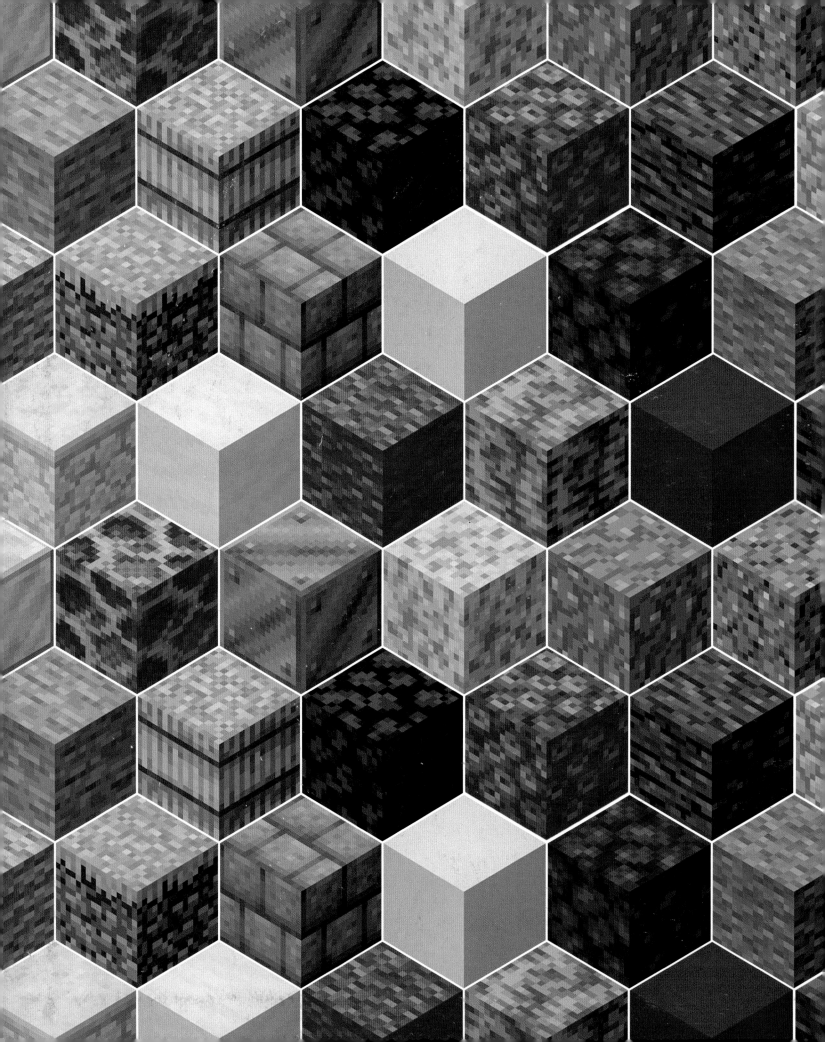